Praise for
God and the Gay Christian

"For anyone who wants to know why some evangelicals find that the Bible does not condemn same-gender marriage, Matthew Vines's book answers the question. Christians who oppose gay marriage should consider what he has to say."

—Tony Campolo, professor emeritus, Eastern University;
author of *Red Letter Christians*

"Many people believe you can *either* hold a high view of Scripture *or* affirm gay relationships, but not both. Matthew Vines proves them wrong. Provocative and relentlessly Bible-focused, *God and the Gay Christian* offers hope and insight for Christians who have felt conflicted on matters of sexuality."

—Justin Lee, author of *Torn: Rescuing the Gospel from the Gays-vs.-Christians Debate*

"A must-read for all Christians, but especially parents. Matthew Vines brings great insight and wisdom to the conversation so urgently needed by today's church. *God and the Gay Christian* has the information I was searching for when my son, Tyler Clementi, came out to me. This book will have a great impact on families, freeing parents of misunderstandings about their LGBT children while letting them hold securely to their faith."

—Jane Clementi, co-founder of The Tyler Clementi Foundation

"Matthew Vines has accomplished a rare feat in this book, combining a detailed mastery of a wide range of material from the ancient world and the Christian tradition, a clear and articulate writing style, a deep commitment to his Christian faith, and an incisive judgment that can cut through complex arguments and mountains of data, and identify the core issues and their implications for human life. This book makes significant contributions, not only to ongoing scholarly conversations but also to the average person who wants to probe more deeply how to think about God and the gay Christian. It is the breadth of his reach and the integrated character of his vision that makes this book particularly worth reading."

> —JAMES BROWNSON, James and Jean Cook Professor
> of New Testament, Western Theological Seminary; author
> of *Bible, Gender, Sexuality*

"*God and the Gay Christian* is a game changer. Winsome, accessible, and carefully researched, every page is brought to life by the author's clear love for Scripture and deep, persistent faith. With this book, Matthew Vines emerges as one of my generation's most important Christian leaders, not only on matters of sexuality but also on what it means to follow Jesus with wisdom, humility, and grace. Prepare to be challenged and enlightened, provoked and inspired. Read with an open heart and mind, and you are bound to be changed."

> —RACHEL HELD EVANS, author of *A Year of Biblical Woman-*
> *hood* and *Faith Unraveled*

"Few things in today's world divide churches and Christian communities more deeply than the issue of homosexuality. What lies at the very heart of the matter is the Bible and its interpretation. The very few biblical verses that touch upon same-sex-related matters say nothing about love and enduring relationships between people of the same sex—on the contrary, these texts condemn harshly the activities they describe, such as attempted rape, debauchery, or depriving a person of his male honor. This has led theologically conservative Christians to condemn altogether what is today called 'homosexuality.' As the consequence of such an interpretation of the authoritative Scripture, hundreds of thousands of members of Christian communities have faced the difficulty, if not impossibility, to live out their non-heterosexual orientation while maintaining their Christian identity. Matthew Vines dedicates his book to 'all those who have suffered in silence for so long.' He reads the Bible and biblical scholarship as an evangelical gay Christian, giving a voice both to the biblical texts and its readers. He takes seriously the biblical text that for him represents the authoritative Word of God, historical scholarship that reads the biblical text against what can be known of its historical context, and the experiences of Christians who read the Bible today. Importantly, his own personal voice is to be heard throughout the book, which only adds to its credibility. A careful scrutiny of the six biblical passages that somehow address same-sex behavior leads Vines to make a compelling argument against mandatory celibacy for gay Christians. More than that, he argues that Christians who affirm the full authority of Scripture can also affirm committed, monogamous same-sex relationships. Matthew Vines's well-read and well-argued book deserves to be read not only by all those who have suffered in silence, but also by members and ministers of Christian communities struggling with the recognition and appreciation of their gay members."

—MARTTI NISSINEN, professor of Old Testament Studies, University of Helsinki; author of *Homoeroticism in the Biblical World: A Historical Perspective*

"Matthew Vines lives at an intersection of identities: a committed, theologically conservative Christian, who also happens to be an out gay man. In offering both a scholarly and profoundly personal reconciliation of a duality often depicted as hopelessly at odds, he performs a public service that is valiant, hopeful, and long overdue. He points the way forward for all those still stranded at the intersection."

—LEONARD PITTS JR., Pulitzer Prize–winning columnist;
author of *Freeman*

"Matthew Vines brings within reach of non-specialists the rich store of scholarly work on what Scripture does and does not say about same-sex relationships. Coupled with his poignant descriptions of the damage done by traditional exclusionary interpretations, his book is an essential resource for all who seek to find their bearings in the current debate over the Bible's teachings for gay people."

—DR. MARK ACHTEMEIER, Presbyterian theologian;
author of *The Bible's Yes to Same-Sex Marriage*

The Biblical Case in
Support of Same-Sex
Relationships

GOD AND THE GAY CHRISTIAN

MATTHEW VINES

CONVERGENT
BOOKS

GOD AND THE GAY CHRISTIAN
PUBLISHED BY CONVERGENT BOOKS

To all those who have suffered in silence for so long

Contents

Reclaiming Our Light— an Introduction

I grew up singing a chorus in Sunday school about how we should share the light of our faith with the world. *"This little light of mine, I'm gonna let it shine,"* we sang in the classrooms at my family's church in Wichita, Kansas. *"Hide it under a bushel? No! I'm gonna let it shine."*

That was before I knew I was gay.

Unfortunately, in recent years, many outside the church haven't been able to see our faith's light due to the rancor toward lesbian, gay, bisexual, and transgender (LGBT) people. Increasingly, young believers in particular feel caught in and repulsed by an often meanspirited theological debate about sexual orientation. They long for a charitable yet biblically sound message on this topic that's not at odds with the Jesus of the Gospels. Most young people today, it seems, know someone who has been rejected by family, friends, or church after coming out. Citing chapter and verse, evangelical Christians have typically offered a response like this to the gay believers in their midst: "We love you. It's your sin we hate."

To be fair, many Christians now support same-sex relationships. But those who do tend to see Scripture as a helpful but dated guidebook, not as the final authority on questions of morality and doctrine.

That is not my view of Scripture.

Like most theologically conservative Christians, I hold what is often called a "high view" of the Bible. That means I believe all of Scripture is inspired by God and authoritative for my life. While some parts of the Bible address cultural norms that do not directly apply to modern societies, all of Scripture is "useful for teaching, for reproof, for correction, and for training in righteousness" (2 Timothy 3:16–17, NRSV).

That view of the Bible lies at the heart of our culture's polarization over same-sex relationships. While much of our secular society and many mainline churches have come to embrace gay relationships, the evangelical church has not. Why? Evangelicals' beliefs are based on how they read the Bible, and most evangelicals believe the Bible condemns all same-sex relationships.

Today, that belief is coming under increasing pressure. For years, many conservative Christians supported efforts to change gay people's sexual orientation. Some still take that approach, but in 2013, the flagship "ex-gay" organization shut down and apologized for the "false hope," pain, and trauma it caused.[1] The failure of that movement has left evangelicals grappling with how to respond to the reality of sexual orientation without compromising their beliefs about the Bible's authority.

Not until I confronted my own same-sex orientation did my church's crisis on this issue become a fully personal one. But that crisis—as I will describe for you in the pages ahead—propelled me on a quest that has resulted in the book you're holding.

This book is the product of four years of meticulous research, building on four decades of high-level scholarship. I am not a biblical scholar, so I have relied on the work of dozens of scholars whose expertise is far greater than my own. My goal has not been to break new ground, but to bring credible, often-overlooked insights to light, and to synthesize those insights in clear and accessible ways for a broad audience.

My core argument in this book is not simply that some Bible passages have been misinterpreted and others have been given undue weight. My larger argument is this: *Christians who affirm the full authority of Scripture can also affirm committed, monogamous same-sex relationships.*

Instead of accepting the divide between more progressive Christians who support marriage equality and conservative Christians who oppose it, this book envisions a future in which *all* Christians come to embrace and affirm their LGBT brothers and sisters—without undermining their commitment to the authority of the Bible.

I invite you to journey with me as we take a careful look at the six passages in Scripture that speak most directly and specifically about same-sex behavior. What I learned in my study has changed the views of my parents along with many other committed Christians in my life. Yet I hope the argument I present in *God and the Gay Christian* does more than change minds. My prayer is that it opens up a conversation in the Christian community that is truly in the spirit of Jesus. The fiercest objections to LGBT equality—those based on religious beliefs—can begin to fall away. The tremendous pain endured by LGBT youth in many Christian homes can become a relic of the past. Christianity's reputation in much of the Western world can begin to rebound. Together, we can reclaim our light.

If you are a conservative Christian, that degree of change might make you uncomfortable. If you are an LGBT-affirming Christian, it should give you hope. If you are nonreligious, it might strike you as unlikely. These goals are ambitious, to say the least. But the argument you are about to read is not lightly considered. This is the book I dearly needed when I admitted to myself that I was gay. And it is, I pray, an instrument God will use to help bring healing, reconciliation, and hope to many who need them most.

A Tree and Its Fruit

My knees buckled, my stomach turned, and I felt the strength drain from my body. It was my sophomore fall at Harvard, and after a long week of classes, I had stopped by the campus convenience store. Standing alone in the toothpaste aisle, I finally asked myself the question I'd managed to avoid for years. *Am I gay?*

The answer was obvious—it could have been obvious for years, if I hadn't worked so hard to ignore it. But it was also terrifying. Even though I was going to a school that embraced gay students and living in a state that had legalized gay marriage years earlier, I suddenly found myself feeling hopeless.

Life at college wasn't the problem. The problem was sixteen hundred miles away, in Wichita, Kansas. I'd been at school for only a little over a year, and Kansas remained far more important to me than Cambridge, Massachusetts. But for everything I enjoyed about my home state, most people I knew there made a significant exception to their midwestern friendliness: gay people. My Presbyterian church, in particular, was filled with kindhearted, caring Christians. But when it came to homosexuality, their views were set. If you were in a gay relationship, you were living in sin. Period.

Still frozen in place at the back of the convenience store, my new reality triggered memories. With each one came a fresh wave of anguish.

Take the summer before I left for college. Our pastor had lamented from the pulpit that progressives in our denomination were advocating for the ordination of "practicing homosexuals." Heads shook in dismay and disappointment.

My parents were opposed to the gay rights movement, even though my older sister and I had become more open to the issue. My final year of high school, my sister, Christine, returned from college with the news that one of her close friends had come out. (I'll call him Josh.) Mom, who had known and loved Josh since he was born, was devastated. Dad questioned Josh's judgment.

"How does he know he can never marry a woman?" Dad asked.

"Well, he's gay, Dad," I said. "Why would he?"

"I'm not convinced he couldn't overcome this. It just seems like he's decided not to try."

That night, Christine and I shared our frustrations. "They just don't get it," she said. "Josh marrying a woman would be a recipe for disaster."

I still didn't know what to think about gay marriage, but I wasn't all that fazed by her friend's revelation. The gay people I'd met at school seemed normal enough, and criticizing them for not trying to be straight didn't make sense. Whether it was a sin or not, gay people were still gay, and ignoring their orientation wasn't going to help.

But my dad didn't know any openly gay people, and he had always understood the Bible to be against homosexuality. If God was against it, Dad said, God wouldn't make anyone gay. So even if some people struggled with same-sex attraction, he was confident they could develop heterosexual attractions over time.

Other students came and went from the convenience store, but I stood there, ashen. I stared blankly at rows of toothpaste, thinking about the year Josh came out—and what would happen when I did too.

For Josh, coming out to his family had been agonizing. Our church, he rightly guessed, would not have been any happier to hear his news. Not wanting to subject himself to widespread rejection, he left town for his out-of-state college.

He left church too.

This was a young man who often shared his musical talents with our church, singing and playing original songs in front of hundreds on Sunday mornings. He was one of the smartest kids in high school, and he was voted onto homecoming court his senior year. Now when people talked about him, it was in hushed tones. The sense of shame over what people assumed to be his "decision" was palpable.

Feeling rejected by our church and alienated from God, Josh started much of his life over on the West Coast. In time, he found it impossible to keep believing in a loving God. As he saw it, the God of the Bible required him to hate a core part of himself. Not surprisingly, he also gave up on the Bible, since it had been the instrument that taught others to reject that part of him too. Thankfully, his family came around over time, and they now embrace him. But much of the damage from our church's stance had already been done. Josh's faith, along with the church community that first nurtured it, was already lost.

I walked home from the store that night feeling sick. All weekend, I could barely eat or sleep. Trying to concentrate on my philosophy paper or my Spanish assignment was impossible.

In the days and weeks ahead, I did my best to figure out a way forward. Josh's path—as much as I empathized with him—didn't seem bearable to me. The losses would be too great. My faith had been of central importance to me for as long as I could remember. When I was two years old, my parents bought me a children's Bible, which I studied diligently over the years. One Sunday, while riding home from church at the age of three, I asked Jesus to come into my heart. (I would repeat this request countless times before I made it to middle school, just to make sure it worked.)

My parents nurtured a faith in Jesus in me and my sister, giving us a moral and spiritual anchor as we grew up. Just as importantly, Mom and Dad lived out their faith in loving and authentic ways, daily confirming for us the value of placing Christ at the center of our lives. So even though I was now facing up to the fact of my sexual orientation, my faith in God was not in jeopardy. Besides, after doing a Bible study of the issue the year before, I had already come to question whether God's views on gay people matched what Christians back home seemed to think they were.

But while my faith felt secure, my relationship with my parents—and with our entire church community—had never felt more fragile. Homosexuality, to the limited extent it was discussed in our church, was little more than a political football, a quick test of orthodoxy. The "progressives" in our denomination supported it, but anyone who truly believed in the authority of the Bible, I was told, did not. In all this, the concerns, lives, and dignity of gay *people* were not mentioned. (As more than a few parishioners would later tell me, they had never stopped to think whether there might be any gay people in our church.)

By some strange feat of the will, I had been able to suppress my own awareness of my sexual orientation until I was nineteen. But I knew that wasn't the case for many others, maybe most others. For a young kid who realizes she is gay and has no one at home or church she can talk to, it can be an impossibly heavy burden. For a young man like

Josh, who internalized rejection from our church with barely a word spoken, it can drive a wedge between him and God.

And what would become of me?

Weeks passed. After deep prayer and several long conversations with my sister and with some friends, I realized what I had to do. I packed my bags that Christmas, boarded a plane home for Kansas, and anxiously peered out the window. Boston would soon be slipping away, replaced by the familiar terrain of the Bible Belt. But this time, going home would be different. This time, I was going to come out.

MY DAD'S WORST DAY

Ours is a Christian family story. It is also a loving, loyal, confused church story. There's nothing all that unusual about it, really. But precisely because similar stories are unfolding in countless families and churches today, I want to share it.

I want you to see how sexual orientation and deeply held beliefs are at odds in ways that injure those we love. This debate is not simply about beliefs and rights; it's about people who are created in God's image. Those people may be like you or entirely *un*like you. They may be your roommate or neighbor, your best friend or a colleague. They may be your son or daughter.

My dad would later tell me the day I came out to him was the worst day of his life. His sister had passed away the year before; his father years earlier. But the day I said "Dad, I'm gay" was the worst day of his life. To his credit, though, he didn't tell me that at the time. He hugged me and listened as I nervously stumbled over my words for an hour and a half. Then he told me he loved me.

My mom, too, responded with open arms, but the news was hard for her to hear. She could barely eat for several days afterward, and she spent much of the next year deeply dispirited. Still, I was grateful for my parents' unfailing compassion and love.

What that love would ultimately look like, though, was unclear. At first, my dad wanted me to consider trying to change my sexual orientation. He'd heard of groups that claimed to change people from gay to straight, and he asked me to read some books he had borrowed from our church on the subject. I was skeptical, but I read them.

He read the books too, and we were both struck by how modest their claims actually were. These "ex-gay" organizations, for the most part, did not claim to be changing anyone's sexual *orientation*. They focused instead on changing people's *behavior*. For people who had been caught up in promiscuity, abusive relationships, or drug addictions, changing those behaviors was surely beneficial. But those changes had no bearing on their sexual orientation—and they didn't speak to my situation either.

I had never been promiscuous or suffered abuse. At an early age, I committed myself to abstinence until marriage. That didn't change just because I was gay. I wanted to honor my body as a temple of the Holy Spirit. But I also cherished the idea of one day having my own family, so I wanted to explore whether a committed same-sex relationship could be honoring to God.

As a lawyer, my dad weighed the evidence for the possibility of orientation change. Pointing to Matthew 19:26, he reminded me that all things are possible with God. Yet after reading a fair amount about "ex-gay" ministries, he realized that none of the evidence seemed to show God was changing gay people's sexual orientation. So whatever my path forward might be, orientation change was not likely to be it.

That realization answered one question for my dad, but it opened up a host of others. If heterosexual marriage wasn't a realistic option for me, what should I do? Leviticus called male same-sex relations an "abomination," and Paul condemned same-sex behavior as "unnatural." As much as my dad loved me, he couldn't disregard what he saw as a clear teaching of Scripture.

SEARCHING OUT WHAT THE BIBLE REALLY TEACHES

Six passages in the Bible—Genesis 19:5; Leviticus 18:22; Leviticus 20:13; Romans 1:26–27; 1 Corinthians 6:9; and 1 Timothy 1:10—have stood in the way of countless gay people who long for acceptance from their Christian parents, friends, and churches. I was blessed by my parents' continued love, but absent a significant change for my dad in particular, we were likely to end up stuck in the same place: compassion, but no support for a future romantic relationship.

I shared my parents' concerns about the importance and authority of Scripture. In my view, the Bible can't be reduced to a collection of great literature, stories, and poetry. It's God's written revelation to humanity, as the accounts of Jesus's life and ministry in the Gospels make clearer to me than anything else. Jesus said that "Scripture cannot be set aside" (John 10:35), and since childhood, I've made discerning God's will through prayerful study of Scripture a priority.

But while I'd once agreed with my parents' views on homosexuality, I didn't anymore. Even before coming to terms with my sexual orientation, I had been studying the Bible's references to same-sex behavior and discussing the issue with Christian friends. Some of what I learned seemed to undermine the traditional interpretation of those passages. For instance, Leviticus prohibits male same-sex relations, but it uses similar language to prohibit the eating of shellfish. And while

Paul did describe same-sex relations as "unnatural," he also wrote that for men to wear their hair long was contrary to "nature." Yet Christians no longer regard eating shellfish or men having long hair as sinful. A more comprehensive exploration of Scripture was in order.

I had a second reason for losing confidence in the belief that same-sex relationships are sinful: it no longer made sense to me.

My mom taught her Sunday school students that sin was "missing the mark" of God's will for our lives. But while the Bible helps us understand God's will, neither my parents nor my church referred only to the Bible when I asked questions about morality. They also explained *why* something was right or wrong, and why the Bible said what it did. By understanding the reasons behind Scripture's teachings, I could apply its principles to all circumstances in my life, including those it didn't directly address.

But as I became more aware of same-sex relationships, I couldn't understand why they were supposed to be sinful, or why the Bible apparently condemned them. With most sins, it wasn't hard to pinpoint the damage they cause. Adultery violates a commitment to your spouse. Lust objectifies others. Gossip degrades people. But committed same-sex relationships didn't fit this pattern. Not only were they not harmful to anyone, they were characterized by positive motives and traits instead, like faithfulness, commitment, mutual love, and self-sacrifice.

What other sin looked like that?

The church's condemnation of same-sex relationships seemed to be harmful to the long-term well-being of most gay people. By condemning homosexuality, the church was shutting off a primary avenue for relational joy and companionship in gay people's lives. That wasn't the case with other sins. Avoiding other sins always seemed to work to our long-term benefit.

I'll always be grateful that my parents were willing to take a closer look at this issue with me. But we all needed more time for study, prayer, and discussion with others. So instead of returning to Harvard for the coming spring semester, I decided to stay home. There, I set about finding as many resources as I could to better understand the Bible and homosexuality.

By the summer, my parents were more comfortable discussing the issue, and some of our friends from church had responded with grace and openness when I came out to them. But they were only a small fraction of our congregation's two thousand members.

"DO PEOPLE PICK GRAPES FROM THORNBUSHES?"

"You're elevating your experience over Scripture," a frustrated member of my church told me over coffee. "I don't accept that."

It was June, and my coming out to our larger church community was off to a mixed start. A member of the worship band agreed to meet at a coffee shop. There, he expressed concern about my openness to the idea that same-sex relationships may not be sinful. His study of the Bible had led him to conclude that both the Old and the New Testaments condemn homosexuality. So while he could appreciate my distress over the harm that may cause gay people, he said he could not allow mere experience to override Scripture's witness.

His concern would be echoed by many others. It's often expressed like this: Our experience is a fallible guide to truth. Proverbs 3:5 tells us, "Trust in the LORD with all your heart and lean not on your own understanding." So, too, Jeremiah 17:9 reminds us that "the heart is deceitful above all things." If we simply do what feels right to us, we can be led dangerously astray.

But this principle also applies to how we study and interpret the Bible itself. "All Scripture is God-breathed" (2 Timothy 3:16), yet *our understanding* of Scripture can be wrong. In fact, our fallibility as human interpreters is precisely why I was asking others to study the issue more closely. I wasn't asking them to revise the Bible based on my experience. I was asking them to reconsider their *interpretation* of the Bible.[1]

While Scripture tells us not to rely solely on our experience, it also cautions us not to ignore our experience altogether. In the Sermon on the Mount, Jesus warned against false prophets, using a term that has long been understood to refer to teachers of false doctrines as well.[2] Jesus explained how his followers could determine true prophets from false prophets. In Matthew 7:15–20, he said:

> Watch out for false prophets. They come to you in sheep's clothing, but inwardly they are ferocious wolves. By their fruit you will recognize them. Do people pick grapes from thornbushes, or figs from thistles? Likewise, every good tree bears good fruit, but a bad tree bears bad fruit. A good tree cannot bear bad fruit, and a bad tree cannot bear good fruit. Every tree that does not bear good fruit is cut down and thrown into the fire. Thus, by their fruit you will recognize them.

Jesus's test is simple: If something bears bad fruit, it cannot be a good tree. And if something bears good fruit, it cannot be a bad tree.

The earliest Christians used a similar, experience-based test when making what was one of the most important decisions in church history: whether to include Gentiles in the church without forcing them to be circumcised and to obey the Old Testament law. As Peter declared of early Gentile believers, "God, who knows the heart, showed that he accepted them by giving the Holy Spirit to them, just as he did to us.... Now then, why do you try to test God by putting on the necks of Gentiles a yoke that neither we nor our ancestors have been able to bear?" (Acts 15:8, 10). The early church made a profoundly important decision based on Peter's testimony. Gentiles were included in the church, and the church recognized that the old law was no longer binding.

In the nineteenth century, experience played a key role in compelling Christians to rethink another traditional—and supposedly biblical—belief. This time, the issue was slavery. Much as you and I might be repelled by the notion, most Christians throughout history understood passages such as Ephesians 6:5–9 and Colossians 3:22–25 to sanction at least some forms of slavery.[3] But in the eighteenth and nineteenth centuries, Christian abolitionists persuaded believers to take another look. They appealed to conscience *based on the destructive consequences of slavery*. A bad tree produces bad fruit.

The Glasgow Presbytery in Scotland, for instance, denounced the slave trade as being "founded in cruelty and injustice, shocking to humanity, destructive of the rights and enjoyment of mankind, and of every moral and religious obligation."[4] William Wilberforce devoted his energies to exposing "the most cruel effects" of racism and slavery.[5] New York abolitionist minister George Cheever called upon the "common conscience of all mankind" to defend the cause of abolition.[6]

Neither Peter in his work to include Gentiles in the church nor the abolitionists in their campaign against slavery argued that their experience should take precedence over Scripture. But they both made the case that their experience should cause Christians to reconsider long-held *interpretations* of Scripture. Today, we are still responsible for testing our beliefs in light of their outcomes—a duty in line with Jesus's teaching about trees and their fruit.

A CONSEQUENCE AT ODDS WITH GOD'S NATURE

By way of my family's story, I have invited you to confront the theological and human question that, in our day, goes by various names: the gay debate, sexual orientation, the dignity and rights of sexual minorities, the movement for marriage equality, and others. For Christians, this conversation compels us to look more intently to the Scriptures that first brought us to faith in Christ.

As we have seen, it also brings us together to wrestle with major questions. What is the gospel if it doesn't bring transformation? Where does passionate loyalty to God's revelation leave off and convenient loyalty to long-held interpretations take over? And one more: What is Christian discipleship if it may not require sacrifice?

Over the next year at my church, some elders and family friends I met with acknowledged that their position asks gay Christians to sacrifice something very significant: the possibility of romantic love and fulfillment. But, they stressed, that doesn't mean their position is wrong. Sacrifice is an integral part of what it means to follow Christ, and Jesus and Paul both embraced celibacy as part of their callings. All Christians who do not marry are expected to be celibate—even straight Christians who would like to marry but can't find a spouse.

As one elder said, "It depends on how you look at your situation, Matthew. I know several women in our church who held on to their hopes for a husband for years—maybe still do. But while marriage is a gift that God blesses, it isn't a right for any of us."

He raised an important point.

Much of our culture does promote the idea that our greatest fulfill-ment is to be found in sex and marriage. To the extent that Christians accept that view, we risk idolizing romantic love and losing sight of our first love, Christ (see Revelation 2:4). It is true, too, that God does not promise us easy lives. We are called to deny ourselves, to take up our crosses, and to follow Jesus (see Mark 8:34).

Does that call to self-denial mean gay Christians should view man-datory celibacy as part of what it means for them to follow Jesus? Or should we view that approach as causing unnecessary suffering—bad fruit, in other words—that should lead us to take a new look at the traditional interpretation of Scripture in the same way our forefathers came to question Gentile exclusion and the institution of slavery?

In chapter 3, we will examine the calling to celibacy in more depth. But in the context of our discussion here—experience versus revelation, a tree and its fruit—I want to make an important distinction.

Mandatory celibacy for gay Christians differs from any other kind of Christian self-denial, including involuntary celibacy for some straight Christians. Even when straight Christians seek a spouse but cannot find one, the church does not ask them to relinquish any future hope of marriage.

Those divergent responses point to the fundamental difference be-tween celibacy for Christians who cannot find a partner and manda-tory celibacy for *all* gay Christians. For straight Christians, abstinence outside marriage affirms the goodness both of marriage and of sex within marriage. But for gay Christians, mandatory celibacy affirms something different: the sinfulness of every possible expression of their sexuality.

Jesus emphasized that sin does not encompass merely wrong ac-tions. It also encompasses the desire for those actions. As he explained in Matthew 5, murder and adultery are sins, but so are anger and lust. So from a Christian standpoint, if all same-sex relationships are sinful, all desires for them should be renounced as well.[7]

But as my dad came to realize, while gay Christians can choose not to act on their sexual desires, they cannot eradicate their sexual desires altogether. Despite the prayers of countless gay Christians for God to change their sexual orientation, exclusive same-sex attraction persists for nearly all of them. The failure of reorientation therapy is why the "ex-gay" ministry Exodus International shut down in 2013. It places gay Christians who adhere to the traditional biblical interpretation in an agonizing, irresolvable tension. In order to truly flee from sin as well as the temptation to sin, they must constantly attempt what has proven impossible: to reconstitute themselves so they are no longer sexual beings at all.[8]

As we'll see in chapter 3, that doesn't match the traditional Christian understanding of celibacy. Functionally, it's castration. Such an absolute rejection of one's sexuality might make sense if one's sexual desires were oriented exclusively toward abusive or lustful practices. It makes considerably less sense when at least some of one's desires are oriented toward a covenantal relationship of mutual love, care, and self-sacrifice. For gay Christians to be celibate in an attempt to expunge even their desires for romantic love requires them to live in permanent fear of sexual intimacy and love. That is a wholly different kind of self-denial than the chastening of lustful desires the church expects of all believers. It requires gay Christians to build walls around their emotional lives so high that many find it increasingly difficult to form meaningful human connection of all kinds.

C. S. Lewis wrote, "I believe that the most lawless and inordinate loves are less contrary to God's will than a self-invited and self-protective lovelessness."[9] Lewis's insight resonated with me even before I embarked on my study of Scripture and same-sex relationships. Lewis, of course, wasn't making a case for lawless loves. He was emphasizing the destructiveness of living in fear of love.

Given that we are created by a God who is Father, Son, and Holy Spirit—relational to the core—such a consequence seems at odds with God's nature. We will consider this idea in more detail in chapter 9, but for now, it's safe to say that true Christian sacrifice, no matter how costly, should make us more like God, not less.

A More Accurate Understanding

Paul wrote in 1 Corinthians 10:13, "[God] will not let you be tempted beyond what you can bear." But mandatory celibacy for gay Christians *is* more than many of them can bear. It produces bad fruit in many of their lives, and for some, it fuels despair to the point of suicide.[10] Such outcomes made it difficult for my dad to see how the church's rejection of same-sex relationships could qualify as a good tree that, according to Jesus, produces good fruit.

So instead of taking the Bible's references to same-sex behavior as a sweeping statement about *all* same-sex relationships, my dad started to ask: Is this verse about the kind of relationship Matthew wants, or is it about lustful or abusive behavior? Is this passage about the love and intimacy Matthew longs for, or does it speak to self-centered, fleeting desires instead?

After much prayer, study, and contemplation, Dad changed his mind.

Only six months before, he had never seriously questioned his views. But once he saw the fruit of his beliefs more clearly, he decided to dive deeper into the Bible. In that process, he came to what he now regards as a more accurate understanding of Scripture. He was persuaded by biblical scholarship, historical evidence, and reason. His new views were confirmed by the good fruit they bore—both in my life and in the lives of other gay Christians he began to meet.

In the Sermon on the Mount, Jesus said that if someone makes you go one mile, go with him two miles (see Matthew 5:41). Whoever you are, and whatever experiences or doubts you bring to this discussion, will you walk with me as I share the evidence that changed my dad's mind?

I ask as a brother in Christ—one who has sometimes been hurt by others' unwillingness to listen, and who continues to see fresh wounds open up in the body of Christ. Perhaps you are convinced your views will not change. Perhaps you hope they will.

Either way, I invite you to join me for the journey.

Telescopes, Tradition, and Sexual Orientation

I n December 1614, an influential preacher named Tommaso Caccini rose to address his congregation in Florence, Italy. That day, he launched a blistering attack on a new idea that he said was "repugnant to the divine Scripture" and to the Christian faith.[1] After quoting from the Old Testament to make his case, Caccini said that those who defended this idea were colluding with the devil and should be banished from the country.[2] Those people were undermining core Christian doctrines, he warned, ranging from beliefs about the nature of God to the existence of miracles.[3]

I suspect Caccini would be startled to learn that churches today embrace as truth the very thing he condemned as heresy. But many Christians would be equally surprised to discover what viewpoint aroused such ire: the notion that the earth is not at the center of the universe. Caccini's sermon was prompted by Galileo Galilei's claim that the sun does not revolve around the earth, but that the earth revolves around the sun.

For the first sixteen hundred years of church history, every major Christian leader and theologian believed that the earth stood at the center of the universe. They based that belief on common-sense observation. To the world of that day, the facts seemed indisputable. But as Christians, their certainty was driven by another conviction.

They also believed the Bible taught it to be true.

Psalm 93:1 states, "The world is firmly established; it cannot be moved" (NIV 1984). The book of Joshua recounts how the sun "stopped in the middle of the sky and delayed going down about a full day," indicating that the sun usually moves (10:13). Other verses describe the sun's motion. Ecclesiastes 1:5, for example, says, "The sun rises and the sun sets, and hurries back to where it rises."

For centuries, Christians held to a literal reading of such passages. But Christians did not look only to those verses to shape their views. The question of the earth's motion drew greater significance for them from the opening chapters of Genesis. There, God's creation of humanity represented the pinnacle of his creative activity, after which he rested. Later, the New Testament explains that God sent his own Son to die for the sins of the world. Since human beings are central to God's creative and redemptive work, many Christians thought we must also be at the literal center of his creation. Today, though, you would be hard pressed to find a Christian who holds that view.

NEW INFORMATION, NEW VIEWPOINTS

What accounts for such a radical change in beliefs from the days of Tommaso Caccini to today? The answer is simple: The invention of the telescope allowed people to obtain data about the solar system that previously was unavailable. When Galileo first looked through his telescope, what he saw cast doubt on the Earth-centered view of the universe. From the moons of Jupiter to the phases of Venus, Galileo's observations supported a sun-centered view.

As a faithful churchman, Galileo knew his findings would be controversial, so he wrote a detailed argument explaining how his observations could be reconciled with Scripture. He contended that the Bible used figurative language when describing the heavens, so that the text would be "accommodated to the understanding of every man."[4] From our perspective, the earth seems to stay still while the sun and stars seem to move. Scripture used the same approach, Galileo argued, but that did not mean it contradicted his findings. The biblical authors never intended to take a position on matters of astronomy, he said. They simply aimed to communicate effectively.

Today, we grow up being told that the earth completes a full rotation on its axis every twenty-four hours. But we still talk about sunrises and sunsets as though the sun is moving instead. We communicate more clearly by describing a beautiful sunset rather than a "beautiful rotation of the earth." And when we come to passages such as Psalm 93:1 or Ecclesiastes 1:5, we read them in the same way that we understand everyday speech.

As straightforward as the issue seems now, though, church authorities in Galileo's day rejected those arguments. In 1616, the Roman Catholic Church condemned Galileo's position as "formally heretical, because it explicitly contradicts sentences found in many places of Sacred Scripture according to the proper meaning of the words and according to the common interpretation and understanding of the Holy Fathers and of learned theologians."[5]

For Christian leaders at the time, the problem with Galileo's belief was not simply that it ran counter to *their* interpretation of the Bible. It also ran counter to *everyone's* interpretation for a millennium and a half of church history.

How could those who took the Bible seriously be expected to

suddenly set it aside in favor of a man with a telescope? What if his observations were in error? And an even bigger question: What if the church found Galileo's discoveries to be accurate, contradicting established church teaching? What else might the church have gotten wrong?

Similar questions trouble many Christians today over the issue of same-sex relationships. Before recent generations, no Christian leaders or churches thought God blessed gay relationships. So how can modern Christians change our interpretation of Scripture based on the experiences of gay, lesbian, and bisexual people? Experience is subjective and prone to error as a judge of truth. Why should we not instead defer to the wisdom of our predecessors, especially on something they all agreed upon?

Those are valid questions, but remember that Christians in Galileo's day had similar concerns about the solar system. Here's what I want you to notice for our discussion about sexual orientation: Christians did not change their minds about the solar system because they lost respect for their Christian forebears or for the authority of Scripture. They changed their minds because they were confronted with evidence their predecessors had never considered. The traditional interpretation of Psalm 93:1; Joshua 10:12–14; and other passages made sense when it was first formulated. But the invention of the telescope offered a new lens to use in interpreting those verses, opening the door to a more accurate interpretation.[6]

The telescope didn't lead Christians to reject Scripture. It simply led them to clarify their understanding of Scripture.

In the last chapter, we asked: *Do the destructive consequences of long-held views among Christians warrant a reinterpretation of Scripture?*

We based that conversation on Jesus's teaching about trees and their fruit. Sadly, negative attitudes toward gay relationships have led to crippling depression, torment, suicide, and alienation from God and the church. I suggested that, if for no other reason, those destructive consequences should compel Christians to take a closer look at the relevant Scripture passages.

In this chapter, we ask a different question: *Does new information we have about homosexuality also warrant a reinterpretation of Scripture?* As a starting point, let's review the traditional interpretation of the Bible's verses about same-sex behavior.

DEFINING TERMS: AFFIRMING AND NON-AFFIRMING

First, I want to define the terms I'll be using throughout this book. Labels such as *conservative* and *liberal, evangelical* and *progressive,* and even *traditionalist* and *revisionist* all have significant shortcomings. The same is true of *pro-gay* and *anti-gay.* No labels convey the same meaning to every person, but I have found the terms *affirming* and *non-affirming* to be the most direct, respectful ways to describe the differences among Christians on this issue.[7] Some Christians affirm committed, monogamous same-sex relationships, while others do not.

As we will see, non-affirming Christians today actually have less in common with Christians of the past than many realize. Yet despite their differences, both non-affirming believers today and believers from past centuries are united by the belief that the Bible forbids all same-sex sexual behavior. In that sense, non-affirming Christians hold what can be called the traditional interpretation of the Bible on homosexuality.

SIX PASSAGES THAT ADDRESS SAME-SEX BEHAVIOR

Six passages in the Bible relate in some way to same-sex sexual behavior. Three are in the Old Testament, and three are in the New Testament.

In the Old Testament, Genesis 19 tells the story of the men in Sodom who threatened to gang rape Lot's angel visitors (see verses 4–11). Further, male same-sex intercourse was prohibited for the Israelites (see Leviticus 18:22; 20:13). In the New Testament, Paul denounced the "unnatural" same-sex behavior of Gentile idol worshipers (see Romans 1:26–27). Then in 1 Corinthians 6:9, he condemned the practices of the *malakoi* and *arsenokoitai*, two Greek terms that may encompass forms of same-sex sexual behavior. Lastly, the condemnation of the *arsenokoitai* is repeated in 1 Timothy 1:10. Later, in chapters 4 through 7, we will examine each of these passages in depth.

But non-affirming Christians do not restrict their arguments to those six passages. Like many Christians four hundred years ago who were confronted with new data obtained from the telescope, Christians who oppose same-sex relationships ground their beliefs in what they see as the larger narrative of Scripture. In Genesis, God created Adam and Eve—male and female—and joined them in the first marriage. Jesus referred back to Genesis 1–2 in his discussion of marriage and divorce (see Matthew 19:1–12). The New Testament then closes with a description of Christ, the Bridegroom, marrying the church, his bride, in Revelation 19 and 21. For non-affirming Christians, the Bible's references to same-sex behavior should be understood in light of the positive heterosexual vision we see throughout Scripture. From their perspective, the specific same-sex references cannot be reinterpreted without undermining that larger biblical vision.

GENDER COMPLEMENTARITY

How would same-sex unions undermine Scripture's plan for human sexuality? Non-affirming Christians frequently answer that question with one phrase: *gender complementarity*.[8] As they see it, God designed men and women as exclusive complements to one another in marriage, making the differences between the sexes essential to the meaning of marriage. What those differences are, however, depends on whom you ask. For some non-affirming Christians, the key difference is *hierarchy*:[9] men are made to lead; women are made to follow. Other non-affirming Christians embrace equal roles for men and women, so they ground "complementarity" instead in the *anatomical differences* between the sexes.[10]

From this anatomical perspective, God designed male and female bodies to fit together, as the procreative potential of heterosexual sex makes clear. Even when straight couples cannot procreate, male and female anatomies still fit together in a complementary way. In the words of the most prolific non-affirming scholar, Robert Gagnon, same-sex relationships are wrong because they involve "sex with someone who is too much of a 'like' or 'same' on the level of kinship, not enough of a complementary other."[11] For Gagnon and many others, too much "sameness" is the key moral problem underlying the Bible's references to same-sex behavior.[12]

Even non-affirming Christians who oppose gender hierarchy nearly always believe in anatomical complementarity. Anatomy doesn't change, so if bodily sameness explains the Bible's statements about same-sex behavior, then those statements should apply with equal force in modern times. Whatever cultural differences might exist between same-sex behavior in ancient times compared to today, those differences would be secondary.[13]

If you are like me, you grew up in a community that embraced this view of human sexuality without controversy. But increasingly, even for Christians who affirm the Bible's full authority, the traditional understanding has become harder to accept. Especially for younger believers, the trouble starts when we put names, faces, and outcomes to what the traditional interpretation means in practice.

A More Personal View of the Traditional Interpretation

While non-affirming Christians are united in believing that same-sex relationships are sinful, they do not all agree on the consequences of that belief. Some think everyone is capable of entering into a successful heterosexual marriage. As they see it, if someone does not feel opposite-sex attraction, he should undertake therapy and prayer in order to develop those attractions. An elder at my home church told me, "Matthew, if you really try, I am sure you will find the right woman one day."

That approach has been called "reparative therapy." But as my dad discovered after he studied the issue, sexual orientation is not a choice, and it is highly resistant to change.

Professional health organizations have rejected attempts to change people's sexual orientation.[14] Even the president of Exodus International, a former ex-gay ministry, acknowledged in 2012 that "99.9%" of the people he had worked with "have not experienced a change in their orientation."[15] The overwhelming majority of gay men and lesbians report that their sexual orientation is both fixed and unchosen.[16]

The permanence of same-sex orientation does not settle the moral questions at issue here, but we cannot adequately address those questions without acknowledging it. If you are a straight Christian, I invite you to think about your own experience with sexuality. I doubt you could point to a moment when you chose to be attracted to members of the opposite sex. That attraction is simply part of who you are.

The same is true for me. Same-sex attraction is completely natural to me. It's not something I chose or something I can change. And while I could act on my sexual orientation in lustful ways, I could also express it in the context of a committed, monogamous relationship. But based on the traditional interpretation of Scripture, I am uniquely excluded from the possibility of romantic love and intimacy.

To give you a sense of what that prescription looks like in practice, let me tell you about my friend Stephen Long. Stephen grew up in a conservative Christian home, and when he realized at a young age that he was attracted to other boys, he worked assiduously to repress his feelings. Eventually, after traumatic, failed efforts to change his sexual orientation, Stephen committed himself to lifelong celibacy. In time, he became good friends with another young gay man who was also committed to celibacy. Without intending to, they fell in love. They valued each other so much that they wanted to build a life together—all while remaining celibate. Stephen's attempt to love his friend without violating his understanding of sexual purity became, in his words, "torture." He wrote on his blog:

> It was like being told to paint a picture, then having my eyes
> removed, or being filled with a passion to play piano, then
> having my hands removed. The love was there—it swelled
> within me, a powerful tide that swept me out to sea—but there
> was no way I could ever express it. Marriage was off limits. Any

kind of sexual intimacy was off limits. The hope of being able to share a bed was off limits. The ability to embrace freely was off limits. We were left in the tortured anticipation of a permanent courtship, destined to always love from a distance without ever coming together.

Once the pain became unbearable, Stephen and his friend broke up. As he wrote later, "I was heartbroken, shattered, and entered one of the darkest seasons of my life, with a broken will and spirit."[17] After much study and prayer, Stephen has developed an affirming view of same-sex relationships. But his non-affirming stance crippled him with depression, anguish, and loneliness for as long as he embraced it.

That life is not something any of us would want for ourselves, our friends, or members of our families. So how, I asked my dad, could God want that degree of emotional torment for anyone?

My dad didn't know what to make of the Bible's six references to same-sex behavior, but he was increasingly convinced he needed to study them more carefully. That has been the same starting point for countless other Christian parents who have changed their minds on this issue. It's also why many non-affirming Christians remain reluctant to fully acknowledge the consequences of their position. As Richard Hays, a prominent New Testament scholar, wrote, "Unless they are able to change their orientation and enter a heterosexual marriage relationship, homosexual Christians should seek to live lives of disciplined sexual abstinence."[18]

"Unless they are able to change..." That subtle equivocation may seem like a minor issue of semantics, but it reveals something much larger, and more hopeful: a consciousness in flux. Acknowledging the

possibility that some people may not be capable of heterosexual attraction stands worlds apart from the not-so-distant past—and from the entire sweep of the Christian tradition. Let me show you what I mean.

HOW TRADITIONAL IS THE CONCEPT
OF SEXUAL ORIENTATION?

There are no Christians today who hold truly traditional views on homosexuality. That may sound surprising, even unlikely, at first. After all, millions of Christians firmly believe homosexuality is a sin. How are their views not traditional, given that virtually all Christians before the past half-century would have agreed with them?

The answer to that question lies in a fact just as crucial to our understanding of this issue as the invention of the telescope was for astronomy: in recent generations, our understanding of what homosexuality *is* has radically changed.

For the overwhelming majority of human history, homosexuality was not seen as a different sexual *orientation* that distinguished a minority of people from the heterosexual majority. It was considered instead to be a manifestation of normal sexual desire pursued *to excess*—a behavior anyone might engage in if he didn't keep his passions in check.

The Ancient Expectation: Attraction to Both Sexes

I was surprised when I first came across ancient writings that describe same-sex attraction as an expected—although not exclusive—experience for the average man.[19] (The experiences of women, unfortunately, were recorded far less frequently.) Here are just a few examples, with emphases added:

- In one of Plato's fourth-century BC dialogues, a character praises an athlete who was so determined to win that "he never touched a woman, *nor a boy either,* in the whole period when he was in the peak of his training."[20]
- A third-century BC epigram speaks of a man's interest in both sexes without any hint of surprise: "Kallignotos swore to Ionis that no one, man or woman, would ever be dearer to him than she…. But now he is heated by male fire, and the poor girl…isn't in the picture anymore."[21]
- A spurned woman in a third-century BC poem who hopes to woo back her lover makes the following statement: "Whether a woman lies beside him, *or a man,* may he be…forgetful of them."[22]
- In 92 BC, a fairly typical Egyptian marriage contract included this statement: "It shall not be lawful for [the husband] to bring home another wife in addition to Apollonia or to have a concubine *or boy-lover.*"[23]

In our culture, it would be highly unusual for a bride to fear her husband might cheat on her with both females *and* males. We usually assume people will experience opposite-sex attraction if they are straight *or* same-sex attraction if they are gay. People who identify as bisexual—meaning they are attracted to both men and women (not that they want to be in relationships with multiple people at once)—are only a small percentage of the population. But those modern assumptions were not shared in biblical times. Ancient Greek and Roman literature, in particular, generally assumes that men could be attracted to both females and males. The first-century AD Greek writer Plutarch wrote:

The noble lover of beauty engages in love wherever he sees excellence and splendid natural endowment without regard for any difference in physiological detail. The lover of human beauty [will] be fairly and equably disposed toward both sexes, instead of supposing that males and females are as different in the matter of love as they are in their clothes.[24]

If you're like me, you may be scratching your head at this point. Could everyone in ancient societies really have been bisexual? What about gay and straight people—did they not exist then? Or are modern sexual categories themselves too restrictive, perhaps obscuring a more complex reality about human sexuality?

Experts have debated similar ideas for years, and they have not all come to the same conclusions. Still, I think it is safe to say that some explanations make better sense of the evidence than others. Here is the explanation I have found most persuasive.

SEXUAL PREFERENCE VERSUS SEXUAL ORIENTATION

When it comes to eating and drinking, we have different preferences. But despite the diversity of our palates, we still think of each other as having the same fundamental appetites: hunger and thirst. Our preferences vary widely, but we don't regard even major dietary differences as revealing someone's fixed "food orientation."

Take vegetarianism, as one example. People don't become vegetarians because they are incapable of eating meat, or because meat cannot nourish their bodies. Vegetarians have the same drive as everyone else: hunger. They simply make a different choice based on different preferences. And those preferences can change. You could be a vegetarian for a time but then eat meat again, and your basic experience of hunger would be the same.[25]

Based on the literary evidence, ancient societies looked at sex in the same way. Everyone was thought to have the same basic appetite for sex. People's sexual preferences could differ as widely as their palates, and some people did express greater interest in one gender than in the other. There are even examples in ancient writings of men who expressed interest only in women or only in males (although the latter group was extremely rare). Even then, we can't apply the modern labels of "gay" and "straight" to ancient writings as easily as you might think. Here's why: In ancient times, even if a man expressed exclusive interest in one gender, his peers would not have assumed he was *incapable* of being attracted to the other gender. A man's exclusive interest in the same sex would have been viewed along the lines of vegetarianism today—a different *choice* based on different preferences. It would not have been seen as pointing to a different sexual orientation.[26]

So did gay people exist in ancient times? If I had to guess, I would say yes, based on their existence across diverse cultures and societies today. But even if that is true, that doesn't mean we can label people in ancient writings as gay or straight depending on whether they engaged in same-sex or opposite-sex behavior. The reason why is that ancient concepts of sexuality were not the only things that differed from our modern context. Ancient practices differed greatly too.

SAME-SEX BEHAVIOR IN ANCIENT HISTORY

In ancient Greece, the most common form of same-sex behavior was something modern societies would never accept: a sexual relationship between a man and an adolescent boy, called *pederasty.* As the book *Greek Homosexuality* by K. J. Dover explains, pederastic relationships were a rite of passage for many Greek males. Boys took the role of the passive "beloved" from around the ages of twelve to seventeen, and they became active "lovers" as adults.[27]

Most males who engaged in pederasty went on to marry women, and some who married continued to consort with boys. So their same-sex activity didn't mean they fit today's definition of "gay," as they showed equal, if not greater, interest in women.

In ancient Rome, as Craig Williams described in his book *Roman Homosexuality,* same-sex behavior occurred frequently between masters and their male slaves. These masters, I should emphasize, were no strangers to sex with women. Not only did they have wives, but many also had sex with female slaves and concubines. Male slaves were typically just one more outlet for sexual gratification.

We see that reality acknowledged in the writing of Seneca, a first-century Roman philosopher. He wrote that a slave often "must remain awake throughout the night, dividing his time between his master's drunkenness and his lust."[28] Cicero, too, attacked Mark Antony as being no better than "a slave-boy bought for the sake of lust."[29]

Another common form of same-sex behavior for Roman men was prostitution. Cato the Elder wrote in the second century BC that "many" young men paid for the services of male prostitutes, and he lamented that "pretty boys fetched more on the market than fields."[30] But Roman men were equally willing to pay for the services of women, and when it came to the spoils of war, they frequently made no distinction between boys and women. As Cicero wrote of one conquest, "married ladies, maidens, and freeborn boys are carried off and handed over to the soldiers."[31]

The awareness that most men who engaged in same-sex behavior also pursued women was not limited to Greece and Rome. In the second millennium BC, an Egyptian myth called *The Contendings of Horus and Seth* told of a god who had female consorts but also raped his own nephew in a bid for power.[32] Around the same time, a story called *The Epic of Gilgamesh* described how a Mesopotamian king used both young men and young women in order to satisfy his voracious sexual appetite.[33]

I'm not saying gay people didn't exist in ancient societies. I'm simply pointing out that ancient societies didn't think in terms of exclusive sexual orientations. Their experience of same-sex behavior led them to think of it as something anyone might do. If we want to learn how ancient writings would originally have been understood, then we have to set aside modern paradigms in favor of ancient ways of thinking. No ancient languages even had words that meant "gay" or "straight." Instead, most of the ancient world believed, as Plutarch wrote, that "the passion for boys and for women derives from one and the same love."[34]

THE BOUNDARIES THAT MATTERED: GENDER ROLES

It might sound as if ancient societies embraced an "anything goes" attitude toward sexuality, but in fact, rigid rules were in place to regulate proper sexual conduct. As classics scholar David Halperin has written of ancient Greece, "They were indeed puritans when it came to sex"—just puritans about different things.[35] Their main concern wasn't the gender of one's partners, but the *gender role* that a person assumed in sex.

In Rome, an adult male citizen could have sex with slaves, prostitutes, or concubines regardless of gender, but it was acceptable only if he took the active role in the encounter. If he took the passive role, his peers' knives quickly came out. Plutarch wrote, "We class those who enjoy the passive part as belonging to the lowest depth of vice and allow them not the least degree of confidence or respect or friendship."[36]

Why this concern with active versus passive roles? The answer can be summed up in one word: patriarchy. Women were associated with all that was weak, cowardly, irrational, and self-indulgent. Aristotle argued that girls were born only when something went wrong in the womb. Had the fetus truly reached its potential, he said, it would have become a boy. He concluded that "the female is, as it were, a deformed male."[37] Even Plato, who is considered to be the most pro-women of the ancient Greek philosophers, believed that men who were cowardly or unrighteous would be reincarnated as women.[38]

Since women were presumed to be inferior, nothing was more degrading for a man than to be seen as womanly. Any weak or intemperate tendencies, such as gluttony or engaging in too much sex—even with women—threatened to expose men as being effeminate. And if a man surrendered to sexual passion too often, he could end up developing one of the most shameful vices of all: the actual *desire* to take the passive, "female" role in sex.[39] So same-sex relations were not fully accepted even in societies that tolerated pederasty, prostitution, and sex with slaves. They were approved only when a man dominated someone of a lower social status. Ironically, that means the equal-status gay marriages we see today would not have been accepted in most of the ancient world. So much for the so-called tolerance of the Greeks and Romans.

Gender roles were not the only concern of ancient societies when it came to sex. And like today, not all people and groups thought alike. For a group called the Stoics, the most important consideration was that all sexual acts should be open to procreation. Engaging in sex outside of that narrow scope was seen in their circles as a product of passion—not in the modern sense of a strong commitment to something, but in the ancient sense of lacking self-control. As the ancient Greek philosopher Zeno defined it, passion is an "irrational and unnatural movement in the soul...[an] impulse in excess."[40]

SAME-SEX RELATIONS AS EXCESS, NOT ORIENTATION

That view of passion, shaped by concerns about gender roles and pro-creation, led more conservative moralists to see same-sex behavior itself as stemming from an "impulse in excess." In his dialogue *Laws,* Plato wrote, "The pleasure enjoyed by males with males and females with females seems to be beyond nature, and the boldness of those who first engaged in this practice seems to have arisen out of an inability to control pleasure."[41] Plato's label "beyond nature" (also translated as "un-natural") would stick, as would the understanding that same-sex behavior was an extreme to which any lustful person might succumb.

We see that concept of same-sex relations in the writing of Muso-nius Rufus, a first-century Roman philosopher who connected same-sex activity to general luxury and immoderation. "Not the least signifi-cant part of the life of luxury and self-indulgence lies also in sexual excess," he wrote. "For example, those who lead such a life crave a vari-ety of loves, not only lawful but unlawful ones as well, not women alone but also men; sometimes they pursue one love and sometimes another, and not being satisfied with those which are available, pursue those which are rare and inaccessible."[42]

The fact that societies of the biblical world associated same-sex relations with sexual excess rather than sexual orientation has been conceded even by a number of non-affirming scholars. In the words of

Richard Hays, sexual orientation "is a modern idea of which there is no trace either in the [New Testament] or in any other Jewish or Christian writings in the ancient world.… The usual supposition of writers during the Hellenistic period was that homosexual behavior was the result of insatiable lust seeking novel and more challenging forms of self-gratification."[43]

In the fourth century, the Christian writer and bishop John Chrysostom compared the drive toward same-sex behavior to excessive hunger and thirst. He wrote that it "comes of an exorbitancy which endures not to abide within its proper limits."[44]

Even a millennium later, the same view continued to hold sway. In fifteenth-century Florence, the Greek system of pederasty had been revived, and nearly half of all Florentine men were involved in it at some point. But most of those men, it should come as no surprise, were also involved with women. In the words of historian Michael Rocke, Florentine pederasty was often "an act of sexual assault and conquest, a spontaneous transgression, [and] a casual diversion to satisfy an occasional sexual urge." It was "an expression of the power adult men wielded over boys," not of a different sexual orientation.[45] So, too, historian Jeffrey Weeks wrote that sodomy laws in colonial-era America were written on the assumption that same-sex attraction and behavior were "a potential in all sinful creatures," not a "particular attribute of a certain type of person."[46]

THE MODERN UNDERSTANDING OF SEXUAL ORIENTATION

So how did we get to where we are today? The modern understanding of homosexuality as a sexual orientation began to develop among an elite group of German psychiatrists in the late nineteenth century. Prior to 1869, terms meaning "homosexual" and "homosexuality" didn't exist in any language, and they weren't translated into English until 1892.[47] Even then, while some doctors began to think of same-sex attraction as an exclusive sexual orientation, that understanding didn't begin to gain wide acceptance until the middle of the twentieth century.

It would be understandable to ask, given the history we just explored, how confident we can be that same-sex orientation is indeed a permanent, exclusive characteristic, and not just a passing idea. But if there is no fixed sexual orientation, then how do we account for the failure of the ex-gay movement? Countless men and women who desperately wanted to change their orientation have failed in that endeavor, even with the assistance of individuals and groups who were fully devoted to the "ex-gay" cause. Yes, human sexuality is complex—far more complex than we will likely ever understand. But even though past societies did not recognize it, the fact is now undeniable that gay men and women exist. Many of them grew up in Christian households, and many continue to place their faith in Christ. The question is not whether gay Christians exist. It's simply "How will the church respond to them?"

Some non-affirming Christians have acknowledged the existence of same-sex orientation, only to argue that the idea isn't actually new. They often point to a handful of ancient texts to support that claim. While this chapter's wide-ranging analysis makes that theory implausible, I have addressed some additional questions in the endnotes.[48] But ultimately, we don't need to get caught in the weeds of ancient texts to answer this objection. There is a simple, clear test we can use.

As I have described, the traditional interpretation of the Bible affects gay Christians in a unique way. It requires them to be single and celibate for life. If past societies shared similar understandings of sexual orientation, we should expect them to make note of that requirement. But they do not. I have not been able to find *any* Christian writings prior to the twentieth century that acknowledge that lifelong celibacy is the necessary outcome for those who are incapable of heterosexual attraction. Instead, all Christian writings before the past century that mention same-sex behavior carry this implicit assumption: even if some people are more tempted by same-sex relations than others, no one is *exclusively* oriented toward members of the same sex.

This means that the church's explicit requirement that gay Christians commit to lifelong celibacy is new. And while some argue that we cannot allow experience to lead us to new understandings of Scripture, our forefathers have done so. Christians made remarkable shifts in their understanding regarding Gentiles, slaves, and the place of the earth in relation to the sun. And as we are about to see, the new information we have about sexual orientation actually *requires* us to reinterpret Scripture no matter what stance we take on same-sex relationships. If non-affirming Christians choose to maintain their interpretation of the Bible on homosexuality, they will have to change their interpretation on something else: celibacy.

The Gift of Celibacy

S o far, we have looked at two reasons why non-affirming beliefs
about homosexuality should be reconsidered. First is the harmful
impact on gay Christians. Based on Jesus's teaching that good trees bear
good fruit, we need to take a new look at the traditional interpretation
of biblical passages that refer to same-sex behavior.

Second, the understanding that homosexuality is a fixed sexual
orientation is a recent development. Prior to the twentieth century,
Christians didn't write about same-sex orientation, so we don't have
longstanding church tradition to guide us in this matter. But even
though most believers throughout history didn't take a position on gay
Christians, they have almost all agreed on the issue of celibacy. For that
reason, we need to give careful consideration to the proposed requirement that gay Christians remain celibate for life.

The traditional interpretation of Scripture, as currently applied,
calls all Christians to abstinence before marriage. But it goes much
further when applied to gay Christians, denying them the very possibility of marriage. According to non-affirming Christians, gay people's
sexuality is completely broken, so mandatory, lifelong celibacy is their
only real option.[1]

Celibacy has a long, honored history in the church. We associate it with Jesus and Paul, with Mother Teresa, and with thousands of dedicated brothers and sisters serving Christ in far-flung corners of the world.

But there's a problem. Christians throughout history have affirmed that lifelong celibacy is a spiritual gift and calling, not a path that should be forced upon someone. Yes, permanently forgoing marriage is a worthy choice for Christians who are gifted with celibacy. But it must be a choice. As we will see, Jesus and Paul both taught this view, and the church has maintained it for nearly two thousand years. Celibacy as a spiritual gift and a choice—not as a mandate—is rooted in three fundamental doctrines, as we will also see: the goodness of creation, the fact of the incarnation, and our future hope of resurrection.

We live in an era when the movement for same-sex marriage dominates headlines and shapes political alliances, leading many Christians to redouble their opposition to same-sex unions. I know from experience that non-affirming Christians want to order their lives in faithful obedience to God and his Word. They also want to honor the wisdom of the Christian tradition on marriage and sexuality. But in fact, trying to maintain the traditional Christian teaching on same-sex relationships *as well as* the traditional Christian teaching on celibacy is not an option.

We can embrace gay relationships and maintain a traditional view of celibacy, or we can change our understanding of celibacy and keep a traditional view of gay relationships. But we cannot do both. Christians who hold, as I do, to a high view of Scripture must decide which tradition to modify. Here, and again in chapter 8 (on marriage), I propose that we make the modification that is most in keeping with sound doctrine, good fruit, and God's nature.

"IT IS NOT GOOD FOR THE MAN TO BE ALONE"

Let's start at the beginning, with the story of Adam and Eve. In the first two chapters of Genesis, God created the heavens, the earth, and everything in them. On earth, God made land and sea, night and day, plants and animals, and humanity. The biblical writer repeatedly observed that, after God made each of these things, he "saw that it was good."[2] Then, after completing his creation, "God saw all that he had made, and it was very good" (Genesis 1:31).

But for everything God regarded as good about his creation, there was one thing he said was *not* good. "It is not good," God said in Genesis 2:18, "for the man to be alone. I will make a helper suitable for him." God put Adam to sleep and fashioned a partner from his rib, creating the first woman. The chapter ends with this statement: "That is why a man leaves his father and mother and is united to his wife, and they become one flesh. Adam and his wife were both naked, and they felt no shame" (Genesis 2:24–25).

This story shows us what the world looked like before it became tainted by sin. Non-affirming Christians generally argue that the creation of Adam and Eve reveals the limits of God's blessing for sexual relationships: one man and one woman. Yes, Adam and Eve were an opposite-sex couple, as was necessary for them to "be fruitful and multiply and fill the earth" (Genesis 1:28, ESV). But the account of Eve's creation doesn't emphasize Adam's need to procreate. It emphasizes instead his need for relationship.

Now, Adam was not alone in only a romantic sense. He also lacked any human friendship or community, which would have made his loneliness all the more profound. But God didn't respond by giving Adam a group of friends. He gave Adam a spouse.

Of course, Eve was not just any sexual companion. She was also a woman, and her gender is relevant to the story. Adam's spouse couldn't have been a man any more than she could have been an infertile woman. The first couple would have to reproduce. It's true, too, that procreation is a matter of great significance throughout the Old Testament. (Although we will see in chapter 8 that procreation became less important after the coming of Christ.) But what's remarkable about Genesis 2 is that, despite the need for procreation, the text doesn't focus on the gender differences between Adam and Eve. Rather, it focuses on their *similarity* as human beings.

When God declared Adam's aloneness "not good," he first brought every bird and wild animal to Adam. Among them, however, "no suitable helper was found" (Genesis 2:20). Animals could offer Adam some companionship, but that wasn't enough. God was looking for someone more *similar* to Adam than the animals were, someone with whom Adam could form a "one-flesh" bond. That had to be another human being.

Adam commented only on the qualities he and Eve shared: "Bone of my bones and flesh of my flesh," he said. "She shall be called 'woman,' for she was taken out of man" (Genesis 2:23). Adam and Eve were right for each other, not because they were different, but because they were alike.[3]

According to Pope John Paul II, the phrase "suitable helper" in Genesis 2:18 and 2:20 literally means "a help similar to himself."[4] Other common renderings include "a help answering to him" and "a help corresponding to him."[5] The Hebrew term for *suitable,* as a number of commentators have pointed out, can also encompass a sense of difference. But that's not an adequate basis on which to import the entire concept of "gender complementarity" we discussed in chapter 2.

Gender isn't the only way a person can be different, and Eve was different from Adam in more ways than her gender. She was also a different person. And the Genesis text focuses only on what these two have in common.

Adam and Eve's sameness, not their gender difference, was what made them suitable partners. There is still more to consider here, from the precise meaning of the phrase "one flesh" to the connection between our creation in God's image and our creation as "male and female," so we will return to these texts in chapters 8 and 9. For now, though, I simply want to point out that the opening chapters of Genesis contain different lessons about the purpose of human sexuality than what many of us have come to expect.

JESUS SAID CELIBACY IS GIVEN, NOT IMPOSED

The New Testament's message on celibacy is somewhat different. Unlike the Old Testament, the New Testament endorses celibacy as an honored way of life. But at the same time, it makes clear that celibacy should be a voluntary choice, not an imposed requirement.

After Jesus told a group of Pharisees that a man may not divorce his wife, Jesus's disciples responded by saying, "If this is the situation between a husband and wife, it is better not to marry" (Matthew 19:10). Jesus then said, "Not everyone can accept this word," referring to the decision not to marry, "but only those to whom it has been given. For there are eunuchs who were born that way, and there are eunuchs who have been made eunuchs by others—and there are those who choose to live like eunuchs for the sake of the kingdom of heaven. The one who can accept this should accept it" (verses 11–12).

Notice that none of the three categories Jesus mentioned describes what we would call gay men. Instead, he described three types of men who do not marry: men who are sexually impotent or sterile, those who are castrated, and those who pursue a call to celibacy.[6] In light of the stringent restrictions Jesus placed on divorce, his disciples suggested they would prefer to be celibate. But Jesus said celibacy could be accepted only by "those to whom it has been given."

Celibacy is a gift, and those who do not have the gift should marry. Some of you may be thinking, *That must mean opposite-sex marriage, because marriage in Jesus's day was between a man and a woman.* Jesus underscored that point by saying, "Haven't you read…that at the beginning the Creator 'made them male and female,' and said, 'For this reason a man will leave his father and mother and be united to his wife, and the two will become one flesh'?" (Matthew 19:4–5). Some argue that Jesus's recommendation of marriage for those who lack the gift of celibacy applies only to those who can enter opposite-sex marriages, as same-sex marriage would have violated his understanding of marriage.

But let me say it again: When we study biblical writings about marriage and celibacy, the question is not whether Jesus, Paul, or anyone else endorsed same-sex marriage or whether they instead enjoined gay people to lifelong celibacy. They didn't directly do either one. As we saw in chapter 2, our understanding of same-sex orientation is uniquely modern, so the question we face is how to apply the basic principles of the Bible's teachings to this new situation.

What we do see in Jesus's teaching is a basic principle: Celibacy is a gift that not all have. "The one who can accept this should accept it," he said, but those who cannot should marry. I would not claim that we should bless same-sex marriages for gay Christians solely on that basis. There are reasons why some oppose gay marriage that we won't explore until chapter 8, so I'll refrain from drawing final conclusions until then.

But Jesus's teaching does not support mandatory celibacy for people to whom celibacy has not been given. If even *some* gay Christians lack the gift of celibacy, we have reason to doubt interpretations that force celibacy upon them.

"Better to Marry Than to Burn with Passion"

What does it mean to have the gift of celibacy? If all same-sex relationships are sinful, might all gay Christians actually have the gift, or at least be able to have it? Paul talked about the gift of celibacy in 1 Corinthians 7, and though he didn't give an objective test for determining who has the gift, he indicated that it's a matter of individual discernment. "Since sexual immorality is occurring," he wrote, "each man should have sexual relations with his own wife, and each woman with her own husband" (verse 2). Spouses should not deprive their partners of sex, lest Satan tempt them to sin due to their "lack of self-control" (verse 5). "I say this as a concession, not as a command," Paul continued. "I wish that all of you were as I am. But each of you has your own gift from God; one has this gift, another has that" (verses 6–7).

Paul never said celibacy would be easy even for those who have the gift, so the mere fact that it is a difficult path for many gay Christians doesn't necessarily contradict his teaching. But it is reasonable to conclude that, for those who have the gift, lifelong celibacy should at least be *possible* without causing them grave damage. Sadly, for many gay Christians, that isn't the case.

Remember my friend Stephen, who attempted to pursue celibacy but found that path deeply destructive? Well, as damaging as it was for him, it was perhaps even worse for his friend Andrew, with whom he had tried to live in a celibate partnership. As Stephen wrote of Andrew:

His struggle had become so intense, so dark, so futile, and so dangerous that he had finally given up, hoping against hope that somehow, God would forgive him and accept him anyway, despite his sexual failings.... I watched him suffer horribly, and I was at a loss to know how to help him. He would call me, sobbing hysterically, feeling miserable and sexually shameful.[7]

There is wisdom in Paul's words about celibacy. While it can be a life-giving path for some, many do not have that gift.

"FALSE TEACHERS" WILL FORBID MARRIAGE

For gay Christians, the challenge of mandatory celibacy goes far beyond their mere capacity to live it out. Mandatory celibacy corrodes gay Christians' capacity for relationship in general. But it does something else equally harmful: by requiring gay Christians to view all their sexual desires as temptations to sin, it causes many of them to devalue, if not loathe, their bodies.

Consider what 1 Timothy 4 highlights in its warning against false teachers who forbid marriage. First Timothy 4:1–5 says that these teachers' "consciences have been seared as with a hot iron. They forbid people to marry and order them to abstain from certain foods, which God created to be received with thanksgiving by those who believe and who know the truth." Forced abstention from marriage and from "unclean" foods is wrong because it promotes hostility toward God's creation.

Even beyond these Bible passages, the question of mandatory celibacy for Christians has actually already been debated in church history, and those who defended the idea in the early church lost the argument. I want to share the details of that episode with you now, as it provides an illuminating backdrop for our current discussion of mandatory celibacy.

EARLY REJECTIONS OF MARRIAGE

You might be surprised to learn that, for the first fifteen hundred years of church history, celibacy was considered to be a calling *superior* to marriage. Almost all Christians accepted marriage, but many thought celibate believers would inherit greater rewards in the afterlife.[8] Note that I said *almost* all Christians accepted marriage. In the early church, when celibacy was highly esteemed, some celibates went so far as to condemn sex and marriage outright.

According to Peter Brown's *Body and Society,* two influential second-century believers named Marcion and Tatian "demanded full sexual abstinence from all baptized Christians."[9] A group called the Encratites added prohibitions of eating meat and drinking wine to the celibacy requirement.[10] Another teacher named Valentinus discouraged marriage based on what he considered the shameful carnality of the body, and his followers sought to eradicate their sexual desires altogether.[11] These groups are often called Gnostics today based on their shared devaluation of the created world.[12]

Today, debates about sex typically focus on how much sexual freedom we should grant, not whether sex is good or desirable in the first place. So it's worth looking at the factors that could have influenced such harshly negative attitudes toward sex. Peter Brown's explanation makes sense. He argued that, with shorter life expectancies and a high infant mortality rate, early Christians associated sex with death as much as with pleasure. That was a key reason why many chose to renounce sex when they embraced Christ's offer of salvation. Having secured eternal life with God, they were free from the constraining cycle of sex, death, and decay. They no longer needed to rely on sex to sustain life, so by committing themselves to lifelong celibacy, some early Christians lived out their belief that death had been defeated. Given that dynamic, ascetic movements were quite popular.[13]

Upholding the Goodness of Marriage

Most early Christians who embraced asceticism didn't condemn marriage, although they did view it as second-rate. But those who did denounce marriage were in turn denounced by Christians whose views became church orthodoxy.

Tertullian inveighed against the opponents of marriage, saying that "hostile attacks" on marriage are "a polluted thing, to the disparagement of the Creator."[14] Christians who forbade marriage, he said, devalued the body and also "denied and doubted the resurrection."[15]

In Irenaeus's second-century treatise *Against Heresies,* he lambasted the Encratites. They "preached against marriage, thus setting aside the original creation of God, and indirectly blaming Him who made the male and female for the propagation of the human race." For Irenaeus, forbidding marriage showed that the Encratites and others were "ungrateful to God, who formed all things."[16]

In the fourth century, Jerome forcefully condemned a Christian who had argued that marriage was of equal value to celibacy. At the same time, Jerome insisted he was not condemning marriage. That was a position taken only by "heretics, who inculcate perpetual abstinence, to destroy, and express their hatred and contempt for, the works of the Creator."[17] Rather, Jerome said, he believed marriage was good, but celibacy was better. "If I have called virginity gold," he wrote, "I have spo-

ken of marriage as silver."[18] Augustine argued similarly, saying, "What
a man forbids he makes evil; but a good thing may be placed second to
a better thing without being forbidden."[19]

Did you notice that words such as *creation* and *Creator* keep pop-
ping up in these quotes, along with a mention of the resurrection? For
the early church fathers, defending the legitimacy of marriage wasn't an
idle theological debate. It drove to the core of a cherished Christian
doctrine: God's creation is good.

Incarnation and the Goodness of Creation

Genesis 1 closes with the resounding affirmation that "God saw all that
he had made, and it was very good" (verse 31). For Jews, that affirmation included the human body, marriage, and sex within marriage. For
Christians, affirmation of the body took on even greater significance as
God became a physical being in the incarnation (see John 1:14). But
Gentile skeptics homed in on the incarnation as an apparent weak spot
in the early church's worldview. God could not become man, they said,
because God was perfect, and to have a body was to be imperfect.[20]

Plato, for instance, had argued that the body was a prison for the
soul and that, after death, the soul would achieve purification by separating itself from the body.[21] The first-century Roman philosopher Seneca also declared that the soul is "in captivity" to the body.[22] This belief
in the radical separation of the body and the soul is often called dualism, and it's at odds with the teachings of the Bible.[23]

According to the Bible, the body is a good part of God's creation,
and its separation from the soul at death is not a cause for celebration.
Yes, death has lost its sting in Christ, but it's an enemy nonetheless—
the last enemy, in fact, to be destroyed (see 1 Corinthians 15).

The Resurrection

It's true, of course, that our bodies are broken. Disease, disorder, and decay attest to that reality all too often. But according to the Bible, such flaws are not inherent in the body, and God will not fix them by releasing us from the physical world. Instead, as Romans 8 explains, God will redeem and renew our bodies, just as he will redeem and renew all of creation. God resurrected Jesus in a transformed, physical body, and eventually, he will do the same for us.

As N. T. Wright argued in his book *Surprised by Hope,* orthodox Christianity has never taught that believers will enter eternity as disembodied souls. Scripture teaches instead that Christians will be resurrected in glorious, physical bodies. Christ's victory over death means that our souls' separation from our bodies will only be temporary. Our ultimate hope—and our ultimate destiny in the new heavens and the new earth—is eternal, bodily life.[24]

Creation is good. The body is good. Sexuality, as a core part of the body, is also good. Those affirmations are rooted in the teachings of Genesis 1 and 2, but as we have seen, they are also necessary in order to uphold the doctrine of God's incarnation as well as our future hope of resurrection.

AN UNTRADITIONAL PROPOSAL

Given the concerns of the church fathers, is it any wonder that many gay Christians who are told to detest their sexual desires also grow to detest their very existence as embodied, sexual beings? It's a sadly predictable outcome—and one without support from the orthodox Christian tradition. With the exception of some Christians now called Gnostics, whose views were quickly rejected as heretical, Christians from the earliest centuries of the church to the modern era have affirmed that celibacy is a gift that can't be forced.

Augustine, in the fourth century, approvingly quoted the prevailing view that "no one can be continent unless God give it."[25] Ambrose wrote around the same time that lifelong "virginity cannot be commanded" and that it "is the gift of few only."[26]

Consider, too, the words of John Calvin, who wrote that "it is not free to all to make what choice they please, because the gift of continence is a special gift." Jesus's teaching in Matthew 19, Calvin wrote, "plainly shows that [celibacy] was not given to all,"[27] so if anyone "has not the power of subduing his passion, let him understand that the Lord has made it obligatory on him to marry."[28]

Calvin ultimately went so far as to say that those who lack the gift of celibacy but do not marry "sin by the very circumstance of disobeying the apostle's command."[29] He wrote that lifelong celibacy is "impossible" for those "who have not received it by special gift" and that those without the gift who insist on attempting it anyway are acting "against nature."[30] Martin Luther argued similarly, saying that "you… are foolish if you do not take a wife when passion stirs and you remain continent to the danger of your soul."[31]

Their words were particularly forceful because they were arguing against the tradition of clerical celibacy in the Roman Catholic Church. But Catholic teaching on celibacy is no easier to reconcile with mandatory celibacy for gay Christians today.

One of the best sources for understanding Catholic theology on celibacy is Pope John Paul II's *Theology of the Body*. Although John Paul II differed from the Protestant Reformers in that he supported clerical celibacy, he also insisted that celibacy could not legitimately be forced on anyone. In his view, even clerical celibacy wasn't forced, because

Catholics who felt called to marriage weren't obliged to pursue the priesthood.

In John Paul II's discussion of Matthew 19:11–12, he wrote that Jesus distinguished between "born" eunuchs and those "who have made themselves" eunuchs in order to underscore "the voluntary and supernatural nature" of celibacy.[32]

Christ's words that celibacy can be accepted only by those to whom it is given "clearly indicate the importance of the personal choice together with…the gift that man receives to make such a choice."[33]

John Paul II agreed that celibacy must be freely chosen in order to uphold the goodness of marriage. The Bible's most important teaching on marriage, as we will see in chapter 8, is that marriage is a model of Christ's relationship with the church. Marriage serves as a temporary foretaste of our eternal union with Christ. But marriage is not eternal. It's merely a sign pointing us to our ultimate destination (see Matthew 22:23–33).

The married state must be affirmed as an image of our ultimate union with Christ. But the celibate state, when properly undertaken, is not a rejection of marriage or sexuality. It's a *fulfillment* of them. The celibate Christian, according to John Paul II, should not reject his sexuality as something shameful. He should choose to orient it more directly toward his ultimate marriage to Christ. By living out daily the true meaning of marriage, celibate Christians both affirm its goodness and remind married couples of its deepest meaning.[34]

Karl Barth, a leading Protestant theologian of the twentieth century, wrote that "a suspicion of or discrimination against sexual life" is not a valid reason to avoid marriage.[35] Marriage and sex are good parts of God's creation. Celibacy can fulfill them only by affirming them, not by condemning them.[36]

UNDERMINING THE MEANING OF CELIBACY

Where does this discussion leave us? The debate about gay Christians requires us to do one of two things: change our understanding of celibacy or change our understanding of marriage. In order to discern which change we should make, we need a fuller understanding of both celibacy and marriage, as the Bible and Christian orthodoxy have viewed them. The purpose of celibacy, as we've seen in this chapter, is to affirm the basic goodness of sex and marriage by pointing to the relationship they prefigure: the union of Christ and the church.

Mandatory celibacy for gay Christians does not fulfill that purpose. It undermines it. It sends the message to gay Christians that their sexual selves are inherently shameful. It's not a fulfillment of sexuality for gay Christians, but a rejection of it.

It remains to be seen whether same-sex marriage can fulfill the meaning of Christian marriage, a topic we will take up in chapter 8. But non-affirming beliefs about homosexuality undermine the meaning of Christian celibacy. Along with the bad fruit those beliefs have caused and the new information we have about sexual orientation, that realization should lead us back to Scripture with humble hearts and open minds. I hope you'll join me as we journey through the Bible, starting in Genesis 19 with the story of two cities that have come to stand for sexual sin: Sodom and Gomorrah.

The Real Sin of Sodom

In many discussions of sexual orientation, it's hard to avoid the Old Testament story of Sodom and Gomorrah. The story is so influential, in fact, that the city name Sodom was used to coin pejorative words for those who engage in same-sex behavior. When I was discussing the Bible's teachings on sexuality with my dad, at one point, he turned to Genesis 19 and read, "Where are the men who came to you tonight? Bring them out to us so that we can have sex with them" (verse 5). He paused, letting the words sink in.

I was in high school, and I had just asked my dad why Christians oppose gay rights. He said it had to do with God's reaction to the men of Sodom. They wanted to have sex with other men, so God destroyed them.

For him, the evidence was compelling. True, he didn't know any gay couples, so he tended to read any biblical references to same-sex behavior as sweeping statements about homosexuality itself. But plenty of other people also assumed the Sodom story was about homosexuality. And it's true that the men of Sodom did ask to have sex with other men.

But I had started to meet gay people at school, and I couldn't make a connection between them and this story of threatened violence and coercion. I wondered if the story might have other things to teach us.

A few years later, when I studied the text more carefully, the answer seemed obvious. Decades ago, biblical scholars on both sides of the issue dismissed the idea that homosexuality was the sin of Sodom. Yet that belief still pervades our broader cultural consciousness, fueling negative attitudes toward gay people among Christians and negative attitudes toward the Bible among gay people.

The account is disturbing, no matter how you read it. A vicious mob surrounded a house, demanding that its guests be delivered for their sexual use. In hopes that he could spare his guests, the man living in the house offered his virgin daughters to the mob instead.

As painful and morally troubling as the story is to contemplate, it raises important questions that we need to answer. What exactly was the sin of Sodom? Does Scripture teach that Sodom and Gomorrah were destroyed because of God's wrath against same-sex relations? And if not, how have so many people come to believe that for so long?

Whatever your assumptions and expectations, let's take a fresh look at this passage.

TWO CITIES DESTROYED, BUT WHY?

We meet the men of Sodom in Genesis 19, but the Bible first mentions their city several chapters earlier.[1] In Genesis 13, Abram (later to be renamed Abraham) and his nephew Lot parted ways in order to avoid disputes between their herdsmen, and Lot moved near Sodom, in the valley of the Jordan. Scripture tells us that "the men of Sodom were wicked and were sinning greatly against the LORD" (Genesis 13:13, NIV 1984). But the nature of their sin is not specified.

The story picks up five chapters later. In Genesis 18, God and two angels appeared in human form, standing near Abraham and his wife

Sarah's tent. Abraham hurried to meet them, bowing low to the ground. Although the men were strangers, Abraham introduced himself as their servant and addressed them as "lord." He had water brought for the washing of their feet, and he helped Sarah and a servant prepare a choice meal.

In short, Abraham was a model host. As John Calvin put it in his commentary on the passage, Genesis 18 highlights "the hospitality of the holy man."[2] Hebrews 13:2 recalls Abraham's actions when it instructs, "Do not forget to show hospitality to strangers, for by so doing some people have shown hospitality to angels without knowing it."

Abraham showed lavish hospitality to his guests, and he then received word of a long-awaited gift: God promised him and Sarah a son. God then told Abraham of his plans to destroy Sodom and Gomorrah. "The outcry against Sodom and Gomorrah is so great and their sin so grievous that I will go down and see if what they have done is as bad as the outcry that has reached me. If not, I will know" (Genesis 18:20–21).

Abraham bargained with God, begging him not to "sweep away the righteous with the wicked" (Genesis 18:23). The chapter closes with God agreeing not to destroy the city if he could find even ten righteous people there.

At the start of Genesis 19, the same two angels arrived in Sodom, still in the form of men. Lot showed them hospitality, just as Abraham had. He bowed to them, addressed them as "lords," and called himself their servant. Lot then invited them to his home so they could wash their feet and rest for the night. They declined his offer at first, but Lot insisted, so they joined him at his home, where he prepared a meal.

The night, however, did not end well. As Genesis 19:4–5 recounts, "Before they had gone to bed, all the men from every part of the city of

Sodom—both young and old—surrounded the house. They called to Lot, 'Where are the men who came to you tonight? Bring them out to us so that we can have sex with them.'"

Lot told the men, "No, my friends. Don't do this wicked thing. Look, I have two daughters who have never slept with a man. Let me bring them out to you, and you can do what you like with them. But don't do anything to these men, for they have come under the protection of my roof" (verses 7–8).

Lot's response angered the men, who replied, "This fellow [Lot] came here as a foreigner, and now he wants to play the judge! We'll treat you worse than them" (verse 9). The men of Sodom tried to break down the door, but the angels struck them with blindness, thwarting the attack.

The angels then told Lot to flee the city, because "the outcry to the LORD against its people is so great that he has sent us to destroy it" (verse 13). Lot and his family left, and God destroyed Sodom and Gomorrah with fire and brimstone—a cataclysmic event that has come to stand for divine judgment against same-sex relations.

But as we're about to see, the biblical text does not justify this interpretation.

THE OLD TESTAMENT VIEW OF SODOM

Christians generally hold that any sin, no matter what its earthly consequences, is equally effective in separating us from a holy God. In practice, though, Christians often honor a hierarchy of sins. Gossip, gluttony, and selfishness tend to attract little negative attention. But sexual sins—especially when they are known publicly—are likely to be met with vocal opposition. This might begin to explain why it's difficult for some Christians to accept that the sin of Sodom had far more to do with a lack of hospitality and a bent toward violence than with any sexual designs the men had on Lot's visitors. It's hard for many of us to work up a great deal of energy in opposing arrogance, a lack of generosity toward the poor, and inhospitality.

This story is important, as we have seen. So we need to understand the intent of the biblical writers in telling it. Let's read the text more closely to see what it was that provoked God's judgment and resulted in the destruction of these two cities.

Evidence from the Old Testament

In the minds of ancient Israelites, Sodom and Gomorrah were emblematic of evil and injustice. The two cities are mentioned thirteen times in the Old Testament following Genesis 19. The references emphasize the cities' wickedness and raise the specter of God's wrath against disobedient people.[3]

Isaiah, for example, castigated Judah as a "sinful nation," comparing it to the "rulers of Sodom" and the "people of Gomorrah" (Isaiah 1:4, 10). But the sins that Isaiah highlighted were not of a sexual nature. They were sins of oppressing marginalized groups, murder, and theft. Isaiah later prophesied that "the pride and glory of the Babylonians… will be overthrown by God like Sodom and Gomorrah" (13:19).

Jeremiah declared that the adultery, idolatry, and power abuses of false prophets rendered them "all like Sodom" (Jeremiah 23:14). After Jerusalem's fall to Babylonia, the writer of Lamentations said that "the punishment of my people is greater than that of Sodom" (Lamentations 4:6). Amos and Zephaniah, too, invoke Sodom to describe God's judgment on those who "oppress the poor" or exhibit prideful and mocking behavior (Amos 4:1–11; Zephaniah 2:8–11).

Of the thirteen references to Sodom in the Old Testament following Genesis 19, Ezekiel 16:49–50 offers the most detailed description of the city's sins. In that passage, God stated, "Now this was the sin of your sister Sodom: She and her daughters were arrogant, overfed, and unconcerned; they did not help the poor and needy. They were haughty and did detestable things before me. Therefore, I did away with them as you have seen."[4]

Sexuality goes unmentioned, both in the Ezekiel passage and in every other Old Testament reference to Sodom following Genesis 19. If Sodom's sin had indeed been same-sex behavior, it's highly unlikely that every written discussion of the city for centuries following its destruction would fail to mention that.

Traditionally, the writing of Genesis has been dated to around 1400 BC. But as we will soon see, no Jewish literature explicitly connected Sodom to same-sex behavior until the first century AD. Other ancient Jewish texts discussed Sodom, but they didn't link the city to same-sex relations.[5]

Evidence from Other Ancient Jewish Literature

In several books composed between the second and first centuries BC, Sodom's sin was declared to be arrogance and inhospitality. Sirach 16:8 states that God loathed the people of Sodom "on account of their arrogance," and 3 Maccabees 2:5 charges them with having "acted arrogantly." Wisdom 19:15 places greater emphasis on a lack of hospitality, teaching that God punished Sodom "for having received strangers with hostility."[6]

The fact that no Jewish writings on Sodom prior to the first century connected the city's sins to same-sex behavior may surprise modern readers. But the original understanding of the story, focusing on oppression and inhospitality, has a much stronger basis in the text.

Gang Rape, Not Sexual Attraction

The men of Sodom demanded that Lot bring out his guests so that the men could have sex with them. But this was not an expression of sexual desire. It was a threatened gang rape. In the ancient world, for a man to be raped was considered the ultimate degradation. As we saw in chapter 2, men seeking to shame a conquered foe often would rape him in order to complete his humiliation. Aggression and dominance were the motives in these situations, not sexual attraction.[7]

That fact is made clear in the Bible, in a passage in Judges 19 that is remarkably similar to the Sodom story of Genesis 19. In the Judges story, a Levite and his concubine rested from their travels in the city of Gibeah. Inns were rare in those days, so most travelers depended on the hospitality of strangers for food, lodging, and basic protection.[8]

In Gibeah, the Levite and his concubine waited in the city square, but no one offered them lodging. Finally, an old man from another region who lived in Gibeah welcomed them into his home. But while they were eating and drinking inside, "some of the wicked men of the city surrounded the house" and shouted to the old man, "Bring out the man who came to your house so we can have sex with him" (Judges 19:22).

The owner of the house responded, "No, my friends, don't be so vile. Since this man is my guest, don't do this outrageous thing" (verse 23). Instead, he offered two women to the men—the man's virgin daughter and the Levite's concubine. Horrifyingly, the mob raped the Levite's concubine until she died.

In Judges 20:5, the Levite said, "During the night the men of

Gibeah came after me and surrounded the house, intending to kill me." The men had demanded sex, but the Levite knew they were not motivated by sexual desire. The men of Gibeah wanted to gang rape and murder him.

The men of Sodom were blinded by the angels before they could break down Lot's door, but the events of Judges 19 give us a clear picture of their intentions. They were not expressing sexual interest in Lot's guests. They were seeking to rape, and possibly kill, his guests as a show of hostility and dominance.

Gender and Hospitality

Even so, the gang rape would at least ostensibly have been same-sex. Some non-affirming Christians argue that the same-sex aspect of the threat contributed to God's decision to destroy Sodom.

In chapter 3, we saw that the idea of "gender complementarity" is not explicit in the account of the creation of Adam and Eve. (Complementarity is the reason most non-affirming Christians oppose same-sex relationships.) But do any biblical texts that directly mention same-sex behavior describe it as a violation of God's complementary design for men and women?

In the case of Genesis 19, the first of the six passages we will study, the answer is no. When Lot rebuked the men of Sodom for threatening to rape his visitors, he gave them a reason to back off. He said, "Don't do anything to these men, *for* they have come under the protection of my roof" (Genesis 19:8). The old man in Judges 19 made the same argument. "*Since* this man is my guest," the old man said, "don't do this outrageous thing" (Judges 19:23).

What Lot and the old man did *not* say was just as revealing as what they did say. Neither Lot nor the old man of Gibeah said, "Don't do anything to these men, because that would be a same-sex act." Instead, they both expressed the concern that the visitors had come under the protection of their homes. The men were their guests, and the "sacred duty" of hospitality (as one modern scholar described it) was paramount.[9]

More evidence is provided by the men of Sodom, who underscored their antipathy toward strangers: "This fellow [Lot] came here as a foreigner, and now he wants to play the judge! We'll treat you worse than them" (Genesis 19:9). The Bible reinforces the depths of Sodom's cruelty by presenting it immediately following two accounts of Abraham's and Lot's generous hospitality toward strangers. The story in Judges 19 also starts with descriptions of two hospitable households.[10]

But then there is the fact that Lot offered his daughters as a substitute for his male guests. Some have argued that Lot's action revealed his belief that opposite-sex behavior was preferable to same-sex behavior.

His action primarily indicates that defending his guests was more important to Lot than defending his flesh and blood. But it's also true that the gender of Lot's guests played a role—not because of Lot's concerns about the bodily "sameness" involved in same-sex behavior, but because of the greater honor men held in ancient times. As we saw in chapter 2, men in the ancient world were considered to be of greater value than women, which made raping a man a more serious violation.

In that respect, the fact that the men of Sodom said they wanted to rape other men did make their threatened actions more reprehensible to Lot. It also helps explain why the old man in Gibeah offered his daughter and his visitor's concubine to the mob. The issue in both instances is patriarchy, not the anatomical complementarity of men and women.

(The patriarchy we see in these accounts is a far cry from the gender-based hierarchy that some non-affirming Christians advocate today.

Even those who believe men should lead while women should follow are careful to emphasize that they believe in the equal dignity and worth of women, even if they uphold separate roles for women. The Sodom story, on the other hand, reflects the inferior *value* accorded to women in ancient times. The dynamic at play in Genesis 19 goes much deeper than the kind of hierarchical complementarity I described in chapter 2.)[11]

NEW TESTAMENT REFERENCES TO THE SODOM STORY

Interpretations of the Sodom story that focus on same-sex behavior lack a sound basis in the text. Just as in the Old Testament, the New Testament focuses on general evil and a lack of hospitality as the sins of Sodom. Sexual sin is mentioned twice, but same-sex behavior is not specified.

Sodom is mentioned eight times in the New Testament. In Matthew 10 and Luke 10, Jesus sent out his disciples, and he mentioned Sodom in the context of inhospitable actions. "If anyone will not welcome you or listen to your words," Jesus said, "leave that home or town and shake the dust off your feet. Truly I tell you, it will be more bearable for Sodom and Gomorrah on the day of judgment than for that town" (Matthew 10:14–15). In Luke 10:10–12, Jesus again warned of a fate worse than Sodom's for any town that did not welcome his disciples.

Most other references to Sodom in the New Testament associate the city with sin and wrongdoing in general.[12]

Two verses, however, speak specifically about sexual sin. Second Peter 2:7 says Lot was "greatly distressed by the sensual conduct of the wicked" (ESV) in Sodom and Gomorrah, but doesn't specify same-sex behavior.[13]

The other verse, Jude 7, is more frequently cited by non-affirming Christians as a potential reference to same-sex behavior. There, we read that the people of Sodom and Gomorrah "indulged in gross immorality and went after strange flesh" (NASB). The phrase "strange flesh" is variously translated as "perversion," "unnatural desire," and "other flesh," which some argue is a reference to same-sex relations.

But the Greek phrase used in Jude 7 is *sarkos heteras*—literally, *other* or "different flesh." *Hetero,* of course, is the prefix for words like *hetero*sexuality, not homosexuality. Far from arguing that the men of Sodom pursued flesh too similar to their own, Jude indicts them for pursuing flesh that was too different.

In fact, the phrase "strange flesh" likely refers to the attempted rape of angels instead of humans. Jude 6 supports that connection by comparing Sodom's transgressions with the unusual sins described in Genesis 6. In that chapter, "sons of God" (interpreted by many to be angels) mated with human women, arousing God's ire before the flood. Jude compares the stories because the men of Sodom likewise pursued sexual contact with angels.[14]

None of this is to say that the biblical writers took a positive view of same-sex relations. As we'll see in the next three chapters, they didn't. But no biblical writers suggested that the sin of Sodom was primarily or even partly engaging in same-sex behavior. That interpretation would only arise later, after originally being advanced by an influential Jew named Philo.

PHILO'S CONDEMNATION OF SEXUAL EXCESS

Philo was a Jewish philosopher who lived in Alexandria, Egypt, in the first century AD. He was the first biblical interpreter to explicitly link

Sodom's sins to same-sex behavior. His is a late interpretation, given that the story of Sodom comes from the book of Genesis, traditionally dated more than fourteen hundred years earlier. (The shortest time difference would be at least six hundred years, based on a later dating of Genesis's composition.) Philo's interpretation wouldn't become the standard Christian interpretation until the fifth century AD. Still, it became the consensus Christian view over time.

Philo was unsparing in his invective toward same-sex behavior. He first argued that the root of Sodom's fall was "goods in excess"—gluttony, lewdness, and "every other possible pleasure." He continued:

> Incapable of bearing such satiety, plunging like cattle, they threw off from their necks the law of nature and applied themselves to deep drinking of strong liquor and dainty feeding and forbidden forms of intercourse. Not only in their mad lust for women did they violate the marriages of their neighbours, but also men mounted males without respect for the sex nature which the active partner shares with the passive; and so when they tried to beget children they were discovered to be incapable of any but a sterile seed.[15]

Philo was not describing same-sex behavior as the expression of a sexual orientation. For him, it was merely a sign that some people overindulged their normal sexual desires. That's why he compared same-sex behavior to gluttony and drunkenness—a potential temptation for everyone.

Note that the men Philo condemned "mounted" males while *also* pursuing "their mad lust for women." That doesn't sound like gay men, does it? And Philo says that, after these men slept around with males, they went back to having sex with women.

My point here isn't to dispute that Philo took a negative view of same-sex relations. My point is to highlight that Philo's understanding of same-sex relations differed greatly from our own. He was condemning same-sex relations as the excessive pleasure seeking of men who could be satisfied with women. He was not taking a position on the issue we are facing today: gay people and their committed relationships.

THE SHIFT IN HOW THE STORY IS READ

Even though Philo pioneered the same-sex reading of the Sodom story in the first century, Christians did not fully embrace it until several centuries later. Early Christians adhered to the original interpretation of the story, focusing on inhospitality, arrogance, and violence.

Legend has it that Origen, a third-century Christian writer, castrated himself in order to avoid sexual temptation. But even *he* declared the sin of Sodom to be inhospitality toward strangers. Origen wrote, "Hear these words, you who close your houses to strangers; hear these words, you who avoid a guest as an enemy.... [Lot] escapes the conflagration for this reason alone: because he opened his house to strangers. Angels entered the hospitable house; fire entered the houses closed to strangers."[16]

Tertullian, a Christian writer living in the second and third centuries, didn't refer to same-sex behavior when he discussed Sodom either. Neither did the fourth-century church father Jerome. Jerome lambasted the people of Sodom for pride and gluttony, not same-sex relations.[17]

But other Christian writers of the fourth century began to adopt, in part or in whole, Philo's reading of the story. The monk John Cassian identified Sodom's sin as gluttony, but he also said that overeating caused the people to become "inflamed with uncontrollable lust of the flesh."[18] Basil, a Greek bishop, similarly warned against the supposedly universal temptation to engage in same-sex behavior, which he said gluttony makes harder to resist.

By the late fourth century, John Chrysostom argued that, while Sodom was infamous for its inhospitality, God also punished the city for its same-sex transgressions. "The men of that time had a passion for boys," Chrysostom wrote, "and on that account they suffered this punishment."[19] Around the same time, the Christian writer Paulus Orosius said in reference to Sodom that "out of luxury grew such disgraceful passions that men rushed upon men committing base acts."[20]

Augustine backed that interpretation at the start of the fifth century, identifying "males burning toward males with hideous lust" as the city's main crime.[21] By the start of the Middle Ages in the fifth century, same-sex behavior had replaced inhospitality as the dominant understanding of the sin that brought God's judgment on Sodom.

What Caused the Shift in Interpretation?

The same-sex interpretation of Sodom's sin was based on a threatened gang rape, which is a flimsy basis at best. How did Christians from the start of the Middle Ages through the twentieth century make the leap from gang rape to all same-sex relations?

There is only so much we can know about why Christians changed their views that long ago, but it's helpful to look at another, similar development in biblical interpretation. When we look carefully at a similar interpretive shift, we see that the historic misreading of the Sodom story was not an isolated incident.

The story of Onan in Genesis 38 was long interpreted as a condemnation of masturbation. In fact, one synonym for masturbation is *onanism*. Because the Onan story was used to condemn all non-procreative sex, it's relevant to our consideration of same-sex relationships.

In Genesis 38, Judah fathered three male children. His oldest son married a woman named Tamar, but that son "was wicked in the LORD's sight; so the LORD put him to death" (verse 7).

Judah then told Onan, his second son, "Sleep with your brother's wife and fulfill your duty to her as a brother-in-law to raise up offspring for your brother" (verse 8). The passage continues: "But Onan knew that the child would not be his; so whenever he slept with his brother's wife, he spilled his semen on the ground to keep from providing offspring for his brother. What he did was wicked in the LORD's sight; so the LORD put him to death also" (verses 9–10).

Judah had told Onan to fulfill his duty as the brother of a man who died without a son. This obligation arose out of a practice called levirate marriage.[22] According to Deuteronomy 25:5–6, this practice was designed to ensure that a widow would have a son to "carry on the name of the dead brother so that his name will not be blotted out from Israel."

The legacy of Onan's brother was at stake, but Onan selfishly flouted his duty because he "knew that the child would not be his." The passage in Genesis 38 describes an act of coitus interruptus, not masturbation. But the act itself was not the problem. The wicked thing that aroused God's wrath was not Onan's act of non-procreative sex, but his refusal to fulfill a family obligation of great consequence under the old covenant.

No matter. Later societies came to see Onan's sin simply as "spilling his seed." Masturbation, contraception, and non-procreative sex were condemned with "proof" from the Bible, citing Genesis 38.[23] In the eighteenth century, a British booklet titled *Onania* warned that masturbation would cause disease, epilepsy, and death, among other frightening consequences.[24]

Most Christians today understand that masturbation was not the sin of Onan. What's more, many also recognize that masturbation is not inherently sinful. But the historic misreading of the Onan story offers some insights for understanding how the sin of Sodom was similarly misinterpreted.

As we saw in the last chapter, early Christians lived in an ascetically charged environment. Movements advocating permanent sexual renunciation were relatively widespread. Orthodox Christians didn't condemn sex outright, as they upheld the goodness of the physical creation, but they frequently sought to limit sex as much as possible.

The most restrictive position, defended by Jerome, held that sex was permissible only when a married couple was consciously trying to procreate. Admittedly, this doesn't sound very positive toward sex, and it's more restrictive than anything found in the Bible. But compared to the complete rejection of sex that some Christians (now called Gnostics) were promoting, Jerome's view still counted as a defense of sex, albeit a limited one.

Other early church fathers were somewhat more open to sex within marriage that wasn't specifically intended for procreation. But procreation still was seen as a basic, natural justification for sex. Beyond that, sex was highly restricted, even within the marriage covenant.

In light of that history, we might conclude that Christians were influenced by their ascetic environment to interpret Scripture in ways that explicitly condemned taboo practices. In later Christian thought, same-sex relations were thought to be "unnatural" in the same way as masturbation, contraception, and non-procreative heterosexual sex. Each of those practices was understood as going beyond nature's basic requirement of engaging in sex for the sake of having children.

But the Bible never identifies same-sex behavior as the sin of Sodom, or even as *a* sin of Sodom. Even when Christians later came to read it that way, giving rise to the term *sodomy* in the eleventh century, their concept of same-sex behavior still differed greatly from the modern concepts of sexual orientation and gay Christians.[25]

That's why my dad, like many others, changed his mind about the Sodom and Gomorrah story. The biblical evidence he assumed would support his belief wasn't in fact there. He still hadn't studied the five other biblical passages that mention same-sex relations, but he started to approach them with a more open mind, realizing he might have made overly hasty judgments about their meanings as well.

With that, let's look carefully at references in Leviticus to same-sex relations.

The Abominations of Leviticus

I stood in front of my third-grade peers and began to recite: "Genesis, Exodus, Leviticus, Numbers, and Deuteronomy..." Only a few breaths later, I made it to Jude and Revelation. No mistakes! Beaming, I took my seat, leading the next kid to take his turn. The kids in my Sunday school class had just memorized the names of all sixty-six books in the Bible.

If you did that as a child, too, you can probably still recite your way through at least those first five books—the Pentateuch—and maybe much farther. And if you grew up attending Sunday school as I did, you can remember the stories, especially from Genesis and Exodus: creation, the flood, Jacob's ladder to heaven, the Israelites' escape on dry land through the Red Sea, and many more.

Leviticus, on the other hand, didn't come up as much. I tried to read through it at the age of eight, but all I got from it at the time was a headache. It seemed dry and full of strange, cumbersome rules. When I entered high school, I still didn't know much about Leviticus. But I had learned the key fact it seemed all Christian kids needed to know about this book of laws: God condemned homosexuality as an abomination. "You shall not lie with a male as with a woman; it is an abomination" (Leviticus 18:22, ESV).

When I was fourteen, I used that verse to "prove" to a friend that gay marriage was wrong. Today, I realize I hardly knew anything about what I was saying—the context of that verse in Scripture, for instance, or the place of the Old Testament law for Christians.

It's no surprise that I was at a loss when my friend responded to me with verses from Leviticus banning the eating of shellfish and wearing mixed fabrics.

Sad to say, though, that's been the extent of many debates about the Bible and homosexuality in recent years. One side starts by quoting Leviticus 18:22 (or 20:13, which prescribes the death penalty for males who engage in same-sex relations), and the other side counters with verses about dietary laws and bans on certain combinations of clothing. We really do need to go deeper.

First, I'd like us to consider the reason why Christians *don't* follow all the laws we see in the Old Testament, from its restrictions on food to its rules about clothing—and many more, including the death sentence for rebellious children. And then I'd like to look at the Old Testament prohibitions of male same-sex intercourse, as we seek to discern whether and why Christians should follow them today.

THE OLD LAW AND CHRIST'S ATONEMENT

Why do Christians find it easy to disregard most of the laws contained in the Old Testament? Contrary to a popular criticism of the church today, Christians haven't arbitrarily chosen to ignore the parts of the Bible we don't like. The answer, as you may remember from chapter 1, is found in the New Testament.

According to Acts 15, early church leaders gathered around the year AD 49 in what came to be known as the Council of Jerusalem.

They decided that Gentile Christians were not bound to follow the law of the Old Testament. The council made only four exceptions, saying that Gentiles should "abstain from food sacrificed to idols, from blood, from the meat of strangled animals, and from sexual immorality" (Acts 15:29).

Even those exceptions were primarily a temporary means of promoting unity in the early church. By the time Paul wrote his first letter to Christians living in Corinth, he insisted that no food was unclean for Christians, including food sacrificed to idols (see 1 Corinthians 8 and 10).

Sexual immorality is the only prohibition mentioned in Acts 15 that has long-term relevance for Christians. Yet the term used for "sexual immorality" in the passage is generic. And as we will soon see, Old Testament laws related to sex don't always align with Christian views on sexual ethics.

Our freedom from the law, I should be clear, is about much more than one decision made by one church council nearly two thousand years ago. It is rooted in the saving, reconciling work of Jesus Christ. The New Testament teaches that Christ *fulfilled* the law. Colossians 2:13–14 says that God "forgave us all our sins, having canceled the charge of our legal indebtedness, which stood against us and condemned us; he has taken it away, nailing it to the cross."

Christ's death made it possible for us to be permanently reconciled to God. Before then, only temporary atonement was possible through the sacrifices of the Jewish priests. But as Hebrews 8:6 explains, "The ministry Jesus has received is as superior to theirs as the covenant of which he is mediator is superior to the old one, since the new covenant is established on better promises."

The writer of Hebrews continued: "For if there had been nothing wrong with that first covenant, no place would have been sought for another" (verse 7). Hebrews then says of God, "By calling this covenant 'new,' he has made the first one obsolete; and what is obsolete and outdated will soon disappear" (verse 13). Obsolete, outdated, and soon to disappear. That doesn't sound like an endorsement of the law's ongoing authority, does it?

Paul used equally strong language when he discussed the law. Paul wrote about life with Christ in contrast to the "law of sin and death" of the Old Testament (Romans 8:2). He declared that "Christ is the end of the law," and he even branded the law a "curse" (see Romans 10:4; Galatians 3:13, NRSV). "Christ has set us free" from the law, Paul wrote, so "do not let yourselves be burdened again by a yoke of slavery" (Galatians 5:1).

Perhaps the most distinctive aspects of the old law were the Israelites' practice of male circumcision and their detailed dietary code. But in light of Christ's sacrifice, even those central tenets of the law no longer applied to God's people. As Paul explained in Galatians 5:6, "In Christ Jesus neither circumcision nor uncircumcision has any value. The only thing that counts is faith expressing itself through love."

It's true that Jesus affirmed the law in Matthew 5:17, saying he didn't come to abolish the law or the prophets, but to "fulfill" them. But upon further examination, that teaching is consistent with the words of Paul.

Paul said in Romans 7 that the law existed to expose our sin, revealing our need for a Savior. But once our Savior has come, we no longer need the law. We could compare it to the way drivers no longer need road signs once they arrive at a destination.[1]

It's easy to forget how many Old Testament laws we no longer follow. Leviticus 3 and 11, for instance, forbid eating animal fat or blood (see 3:17), anything that lives in the water but doesn't have fins and scales (see 11:10–12), and animals that walk on all fours and have paws (see 11:27). Those prohibitions encompass bacon, ham, sausage, clams, crabs, lobsters, and shrimp, to name just a few. For the Israelites, those foods were all abominations.

And it wasn't just a strict dietary code that the Israelites had to keep. According to Leviticus 13, those with infectious diseases had to be quarantined. They were required to make their condition clear by tearing their clothes and crying out, "Unclean! Unclean!" near others for as long as the infection lasted. Leviticus 15 specifies that any bodily discharge makes a person unclean, sometimes for up to a week.

Among the activities prohibited in Leviticus 19 are planting two types of seed in the same field (verse 19), wearing clothing woven of two types of material (verse 19), getting tattoos (verse 28), and cutting the hair at the sides of one's head (verse 27).

That list is short. If you read Leviticus, you'll likely be surprised at the scope of its regulations and prohibitions. Christ's death on the cross liberated Christians from all that—what Paul called "the yoke of slavery." Which leads to the obvious question: Are Christians also released from the prohibitions of male same-sex intercourse?

In one sense, the answer is an uncontroversial yes. Our standing before God doesn't depend on whether we've followed any laws. But in another sense—whether God blesses same-sex relationships—the answer is less clear. Non-affirming Christians often argue for the ongoing relevance of Leviticus by pointing to the New Testament's statements on same-sex behavior, which are an important part of this conversation. (We'll look at those New Testament passages in chapters 6 and 7.) For now, though, it's important to focus on Leviticus in its own right.

MORAL LAWS VERSUS CEREMONIAL LAWS?

It's true that there are a number of Old Testament laws that correspond with Christian beliefs about sin—prohibitions of murder, adultery, and idolatry, for instance. So Christians have long tried to distinguish between laws we should still seek to follow, calling them "moral" laws, and laws that pertained only to ancient Israel, which we often call "ceremonial" or "ritual" laws.

There is something to be said for that approach, but the Old Testament itself never makes those distinctions. For the ancient Israelites, *all* the laws would have been moral laws, even strictures against mixing fabrics in one's clothing. So even though Christians approach the law differently, we need to bear in mind that distinctions such as "moral" and "ceremonial" are of our own making, not derived from the Old Testament.

That said, we can still help to answer the question of whether Christians should observe the prohibitions of male same-sex intercourse when we focus on the *reason* for the laws' inclusion in Leviticus. I expect you'll recall that "gender complementarity" is the reason why most non-affirming Christians think the Bible says what it does about same-sex behavior. They believe that God designed men and women to be each other's exclusive sexual complements and that the Bible speaks negatively toward same-sex behavior because same-sex unions don't fulfill that intended complementarity.

So the most clarifying question we can ask in this discussion is this: Are the laws we find in Leviticus 18:22 and 20:13 grounded in a view of gender complementarity that applies to Christians? If so, even though we aren't under the law, our beliefs about same-sex relationships should still align with those passages. But if not, and the prohibitions were based on a reason that *doesn't* extend to modern same-sex unions, then a Christian view on the subject might look significantly different.

THREE PERTINENT ISSUES IN OLD TESTAMENT LAW

First, let's address three aspects of the verses that you may have heard mentioned before. In order to defend the ongoing relevance of the prohibitions, non-affirming Christians often point to what they see as the unique nature of sexual laws in the Old Testament, the use of the word *abomination,* and the application of the death penalty.

Do Laws on Sexual Matters Differ from Other Laws?

"Sure," some Christians say, "the dietary and clothing laws applied only to ancient Israel. But the sexual laws still apply to all of us."

Leviticus 18 and 20, after all, don't prohibit only same-sex relations between men. The chapters also forbid incest, adultery, and bestiality, which Christians continue to regard as sinful.[2] However, those chapters also prohibit a sexual practice many Christians do *not* regard as sinful: sex during a woman's menstrual period (see Leviticus 18:19). Leviticus 20:18 commands that couples who engage in that practice be "cut off from their people."

What's more, the Old Testament permits divorce if a husband "finds something indecent about" his wife (Deuteronomy 24:1), but the New Testament forbids divorce in those cases (see Matthew 19:1–12). Deuteronomy 22:28–29 says that if a man rapes a virgin who isn't pledged to be married, he must marry her himself. Christians have never followed that law.

As I mentioned in chapter 4, the Old Testament required the practice of levirate marriage. As Deuteronomy 25:5–6 explains, if a man dies without a son, his brother must marry his widow and have a son by her. But Christians have never practiced that law, even though it was a crucial aspect of marriage in the Old Testament.

Most jarring from a Christian standpoint, though, the Old Testament doesn't condemn either polygamy or concubinage. On the contrary, it often *assumes* them. Deuteronomy 21:15–17 starts with these words: "If a man has two wives, and he loves one but not the other..." And in 2 Samuel 12:7–19, David was punished by God for his adultery with Bathsheba, but he was not punished—or even rebuked—for having multiple wives.

In the New Testament, however, Jesus described marriage as monogamous (see Matthew 19:1–12). We see that understanding reflected in Ephesians 5:21–33, and 1 Timothy 3:2 specifies that men who are church leaders should be "the husband of but one wife" (NIV 1984). So, too, the Christian tradition has always rejected polygamy and concubinage. All this is to say that not all Old Testament sexual norms carry over to Christians.

Is Homosexuality an Abomination?

In the documentary film *For the Bible Tells Me So,* the father of a lesbian daughter from North Carolina described his struggle with her sexuality. He loved his daughter, he said, and in some ways, he even wanted to support her intimate relationship with another woman. But he concluded, "I have to go with what the Bible says. I have to. And the Bible says it's an abomination."[3] That word has proven a major stumbling block to many Christians wrestling with this issue, and it's not hard to see why. It's strikingly negative.

But here's what I want you to notice: while significant overlap does exist between practices the Old Testament calls "abominations" and practices Christians consider sinful, Christians also accept many Old Testament "abominations" without controversy.

Why is that? Four Hebrew terms are translated as "abomination" in the King James Version of the Bible. Of those four, the main term is *toevah*, which appears in Leviticus 18 and 20. It's used 117 times in the Old Testament. In the vast majority of cases, *toevah* refers to idolatrous practices of Gentiles, which led Old Testament scholar Phyllis Bird to conclude that "it is not an ethical term, but a term of boundary marking," with "a basic sense of taboo."[4] Hebrew scholar Saul Olyan and rabbinic scholar Daniel Boyarin, among others, share Bird's view.[5]

Deuteronomy 7:25–26 labels the idols of the Canaanites an "abomination," even saying the gold and silver on the idols were tainted by association with idolatry (KJV). According to Genesis 43:32, for the Egyptians to eat with the Hebrews would have been an abomination to the Egyptians, and Genesis 46:34 says that "every shepherd is an abomination unto the Egyptians" (KJV). The term appears again in Exodus 8:26, where Moses said it would be an "abomination" to the Egyptians for the Israelites to make sacrifices near the Pharaoh's palace (KJV).

This boundary-marking nature of the term helps explain why a number of practices Christians widely accept also are called abominations. Here are a few: sexual relations during a woman's menstrual period (see Leviticus 18:19); charging interest on loans (see Ezekiel 18:13); and burning incense (see Isaiah 1:13). Deuteronomy 14:3–21 contains an extensive list of abominations, including the eating of pork, rabbit, shellfish, and animals that are already dead. So while *abomination* is a negative word, it doesn't necessarily correspond to Christian views of sin.

The Death Penalty

Now, the death penalty, which Leviticus 20:13 applies to males who engage in same-sex relations, is indeed a severe punishment. But consider that *all* the punishments in the old law seem severe to us. Given the threats posed to the Israelites by starvation, disease, internal discord, and attacks from other tribes, maintaining order was of paramount importance.[6] So if a priest's daughter fell into prostitution, she was to be burned at the stake (see Leviticus 21:9). Anyone who used the Lord's name in vain was not only to be reprimanded, but to be stoned (see Leviticus 24:16). Children who disobeyed their parents were also to be stoned (see Deuteronomy 21:18–21).

The death penalty was even applied to some practices most Christians don't see as moral issues at all. According to Exodus 35:2, working on the Sabbath was a capital offense. And in Ezekiel 18:13, the death penalty was applied to anyone who charged interest on a loan.

BACK TO THE ISSUE OF GENDER COMPLEMENTARITY

Although the three issues detailed above are often invoked to reject same-sex relationships, they don't settle a Christian view of the subject. But non-affirming Christians often ground their case in the idea that Leviticus banned male same-sex relations because same-sex unions violate God's intention for gender complementarity.

There are two main understandings of gender complementarity: hierarchy and anatomy. The anatomical view is the most widely held, as many non-affirming Christians actually oppose gender hierarchy. So as we read these ancient texts, we need to keep these questions in mind: Do these writings suggest that same-sex unions are wrong because of the anatomical "sameness" of the partners? Or is the primary concern a different issue?

Let's look at the verses in context and ask whether they speak to the issue of anatomical complementarity.

Same-Sex Relations and the Subordinate Status of Women

One of the earliest commentaries on Leviticus 18:22 and 20:13 is that of Philo in the first century AD. When Philo discussed the verses, he decried what he called the "evil" of pederasty. But surprisingly from our standpoint, the reason he condemned pederasty wasn't the age difference between the partners. He directed his outrage instead at the thought that males might suffer "the affliction of being treated like women."

Based on what we've studied so far, you probably aren't shocked to read his remark. But I want you to notice the close link between Philo's views on same-sex relations and his beliefs about women. Philo called the passive male partner in same-sex relations a "man-woman who adulterates the precious coinage of his nature." He condemned the active partner as well, on grounds that would offend both affirming and non-affirming Christians today. Philo said the active partner was "a guide and teacher of *those greatest of all evils,* unmanliness and...effeminacy" (emphasis added).[7]

That is a stunning statement. If a poll were conducted today about the "greatest of all evils," do you think "unmanliness and effeminacy" would make the list, much less land at the top? "Evil" usually is reserved for sins such as murder, rape, or genocide—not the basic nature of half the human race.

But in the ancient world, deeply misogynistic attitudes were the norm. We see a devaluation of women reflected in many ancient discussions of same-sex behavior. Plutarch, for instance, said males who took the passive role in sex showed "weakness and effeminacy" by doing so.[8]

Clement of Alexandria, a second-century Christian writer, said passive men "suffer the things of women."[9] He warned men against removing body hair, writing that a man's willingness to engage in a feminine activity meant he would take the woman's role in sex. "He who in the light of day denies his manhood," Clement wrote, "will prove himself manifestly a woman by night."[10]

Yes, the clear denigration of women in these texts is offensive. But notice what these writers *don't* say. They don't talk about the design of male and female bodies—there is no mention of anatomical complementarity. Instead, they base their rejection of same-sex relations on a different belief: because women are inferior to men, it is degrading for a man to be treated like a woman.

Reading Leviticus in Its Ancient Context

What insight might this idea give us into Leviticus? Hebrew linguist Saul Olyan has argued that Leviticus 18:22 and 20:13 specifically prohibit male anal intercourse. Olyan based his argument on a comparison of the language in Leviticus to texts such as Numbers 31:17–18 and Judges 21:11–12. In those verses, the Bible uses similar language to describe women's loss of virginity through vaginal penetration. Olyan contended that the prohibited act in Leviticus is the analogous one for men: anal penetration.[11]

His argument draws support from the Talmud, a collection of rabbinic commentaries from the early centuries AD. When discussing Leviticus, the writers of the Babylonian Talmud distinguished between anal intercourse and other sexual acts between men. Only anal penetration of a male is prohibited in Leviticus, they said. They treated other same-sex acts as separate, lesser issues of lust.[12]

If the concern in Leviticus were that same-sex unions violate the anatomical complementarity of men and women, we shouldn't see distinctions like this. All same-sex acts should be equally prohibited. But that isn't what we find, either in Leviticus or in other law codes from the ancient Near East.

Take the *Middle Assyrian Laws,* a Mesopotamian legal code from the mid-second millennium BC. "If a man has sex with his comrade and they prove the charges against him and find him guilty, they shall have sex with him and they shall turn him into a eunuch." The term "comrade" here means a social equal, indicating that the main problem with sex between equal-status men was that it degraded the passive partner in the eyes of his peers.[13] Babylonian omens from the same time period made similar distinctions when discussing male same-sex relations, predicting good or bad fortune based on the social status of the partners involved.[14]

It's true, as some non-affirming Christians have pointed out, that Leviticus doesn't make distinctions between active and passive partners. It prescribes the same punishment for both. So does that mean that social status isn't the concern behind the Old Testament's prohibitions?

I don't think we can draw that conclusion. As we saw above, Philo condemned both partners in male same-sex intercourse, and social status was very much on his mind. He rebuked the passive partner for becoming feminized and the active partner for enabling that feminization. That equality of treatment regardless of role is unique among ancient law codes, but so is the declaration of Leviticus 24:22 that the Israelites "are to have the same law for the foreigner and the native-born." The law treated foreigners and the native-born as social equals, which helps explain why both male partners are condemned. Old Testament scholars Richard Elliott Friedman and Shawna Dolansky have argued that Leviticus prohibited all male same-sex intercourse "since by cross-cultural perception such intercourse would necessarily denigrate the passive partner and violate his equal status under God's law."[15]

None of these considerations lends support to the idea that the Leviticus verses are grounded in a commitment to anatomical complementarity. In fact, the entire question of how bodies fit together doesn't seem to be on the radar. The concern we see instead is centered on the proper ordering of gender roles in a patriarchal society.

That understanding also sheds light on why Leviticus contains no parallel prohibition of *female* same-sex relations. If the issue were anatomical complementarity, female same-sex relations should be condemned on an equal basis. And yet, the text is silent in this matter. But from the standpoint of gender roles, the absence of such a prohibition makes more sense.

While female same-sex relations were condemned nearly unanimously throughout the ancient world, they often didn't draw as much ire as male same-sex relations. This is due to the fact that women did not have as much honor to lose.[16] As a speaker in Pseudo-Lucian's dialogues explained it, "How much better that a woman should force her way into the province of male luxury than that the nobility of the male sex should become effeminate and play the part of a woman!"[17]

PATRIARCHY AND THE KINGDOM OF GOD

Many of the texts we've considered in this chapter are grounded in beliefs about gender hierarchy. But there's a crucial difference between the kind of hierarchy we've seen here and the hierarchy that some non-affirming Christians advocate today. As I mentioned in chapter 4, Christians today who support gender hierarchy insist that, while they don't believe in equal *roles* for women, they believe in the equal *value* of women. In the words of John Piper and Wayne Grudem, "Women are indeed *fully equal* to men in personhood, in importance, and in status before God."[18]

But in the ancient world, women were not thought simply to have "equal value but different roles." They were thought to have *less value*. How else could a father offer his daughters to a mob bent on gang rape as a substitute for male guests? How else could effeminacy be called an "evil" and women be referred to as "deformed males" by leading thinkers of the day? How else, as we will see in chapter 7, could women be uniquely associated with all kinds of universal vices, while the word *virtue* actually comes from the Latin word for "male"?

The kind of hierarchy that shaped the world of Leviticus is of a different order of magnitude than anything non-affirming Christians promote today. So does that mean the Bible is simply a sexist, or even misogynistic, document and that modern Christians have simply closed their eyes to its most regressive aspects?

It's true that much of the narrative and many of the laws in the Bible, especially in the Old Testament, have little in common with a modern egalitarian view. According to Exodus 21:2–11, male slaves are to be freed after six years, but female slaves are never to be freed. Women are less valued than men in vow redemptions (see Leviticus 27:1–8), and they are not allowed to inherit property if they have a living male sibling (see Deuteronomy 21:15–17). The Old Testament applies the death penalty to women who engage in premarital sex, but it doesn't penalize men who do the same (see Deuteronomy 22:13–21). And men are granted the exclusive right to initiate divorce (see Deuteronomy 22:13–29; 24:1–4).[19]

But we can't look at the status of women in the Old Testament in a cultural vacuum and assume that represents the Bible's message about gender relations. We have to look at the Old Testament both in its ancient context and in light of the New Testament's teachings. When we do, the biblical picture regarding gender relations changes significantly.

Patriarchy in Context

Patriarchy was in no sense unique to ancient Israel. It was the standard way ancient societies were organized. Men were granted far more honor and value than women. So the more pertinent question is not whether ancient Israel was structured similarly, but whether it granted greater or lesser dignity to women compared with the expectations and practices of other nations at the time.

Even though women were generally not treated equally to men in the Old Testament, we do occasionally see women assuming leadership roles. Miriam and Huldah were called prophetesses (see Exodus 15:20; 2 Kings 22:14), and Deborah assumed the role of a judge (see Judges 4:4–5:31). Those exceptions don't erase the subordinate status of women, but they are a sign that women's subordinate status may be a reflection of ancient culture rather than a foundational precept for God's people.

By the time we come to the New Testament, women generally still occupied a subordinate role. But again, some women did hold leadership positions, including Lydia, Phoebe, Euodia, and Syntyche (see Acts 16:14–15; Romans 16:1–2; Philippians 4:2–3). And in Galatians 3:28, Paul said something remarkable for the first century. Speaking of those who have faith in Christ, he wrote, "There is neither Jew nor Gentile, neither slave nor free, nor is there male and female, for you are all one in Christ Jesus." By saying that our ultimate status in Christ is not bound up in worldly hierarchies of ethnicity, class, and gender, Paul undermined the belief that patriarchy has a place in the kingdom of God.[20]

Why, then, would we see patriarchy within God's people? That's a similar question to one that Jesus addressed in Matthew 19. Jesus said that, although divorce is not God's will, "Moses permitted you to divorce your wives because your hearts were hard" (Matthew 19:8). As John Piper has written of Mark 10:5, the equivalent of Matthew 19:8, this passage indicates "that there are laws in the Old Testament that are not expressions of God's will for all time, but expressions of how best to manage sin in a particular people at a particular time."[21] That's the same principle Christians use when interpreting the Old Testament's allowances for slavery and polygamy: God working within flawed institutions but ultimately leading people in the direction of his kingdom. Given the evidence we've reviewed, we should interpret patriarchy in the Bible in the same way.

If correct, that view has profound implications for our understanding of Leviticus 18:22 and 20:13. Yes, ancient Israel was dominated by patriarchal structures and norms, which we see reflected throughout the Old Testament—including in its prohibitions of male same-sex intercourse. But not only is that unrelated to anatomical gender complementarity, it isn't even the kind of *hierarchical* gender complementarity some non-affirming Christians today advocate. That's because the verses reflect the inferior value that was commonly accorded to women in ancient times, not just their subordinate status in those societies. But far from being a reason to view Scripture as outdated or sexist, the Bible itself is what points us toward a path where patriarchy is no more.

6

Excess Passion and Unnatural Acts in Romans 1

can't erase what's in the Bible," declares Mary Griffith in the film *Prayers for Bobby.* The 2009 movie is based on the story of a Christian family in California.[1] In this scene, Mary is speaking to her son after he comes out, referring to a passage from the New Testament book of Romans. These words of Paul have long haunted gay people:

> Because of this [referring to idol worship], God gave them over
> to shameful lusts. Even their women exchanged natural sexual
> relations for unnatural ones. In the same way the men also
> abandoned natural relations with women and were inflamed
> with lust for one another. Men committed shameful acts with
> other men, and received in themselves the due penalty for their
> error. (Romans 1:26–27)

Many people point to Paul's letter to the church in Rome when asked what brought them to faith in Christ. They say they followed the Romans Road to salvation. But there is a sad irony here. For countless lesbian, gay, bisexual, and transgender people, Romans is the book that has driven them away from their faith and torn them from their homes and families. It's the book that's sent so many down a path of despair.

For Bobby Griffith, this was sadly the case. His mother's interpretation of this passage from Romans led to so much hopelessness that he took his life.

This passage is not of central importance to Paul's message in Romans. In fact, he used it only as a brief example to drive home a point he was making about idolatry. But in two verses (Romans 1:26–27), he described lustful same-sex relations between men, likely between women as well, and his words were starkly negative.

If you grew up in a church that held beliefs similar to the ones I was taught, you have probably been told that there is a clear choice. We can either affirm same-sex relationships or uphold Paul's authority as a biblical writer—but we cannot do both. A number of non-affirming Christians would even agree with my basic analysis of the Old Testament passages, discussed in chapters 4 and 5. But for most Christians who oppose same-sex relationships, Paul's words in Romans 1 are the end of the debate.

As Richard Mouw, former president of Fuller Theological Seminary, said in the documentary film *For the Bible Tells Me So,* "There's not a lot in the Old Testament that settles the question. We have to turn to the New Testament. The one that's very clear is Romans 1.... Whatever the other stuff in the Old Testament, one thing that carries over as an enduring thing is that God disapproves of same-sex genital intimacy. He does not want men lying with men and women lying with women, denying the natural use."[2]

There's no question that Romans 1:26–27 is the most significant biblical passage in this debate. It's the longest reference to same-sex behavior in Scripture, and it appears in the New Testament. But was

Bobby Griffith's mother right when she cited this passage as a reason to reject his sexual orientation? What was Paul saying here? Was his intent to teach that gay people's sexual orientation falls outside of God's natural design?

To answer those questions, we need to engage with the broader context of these verses. Let's start by looking at Romans chapters 1 through 3.

THE HEART OF ROMANS 1

Romans 1:26–27 merely illustrates Paul's larger point: Turning away from God to worship idols is folly. And even that argument is secondary to his main teaching that opens the book of Romans.

Paul's message in Romans 1–3 is that no one is righteous. All people "have sinned and fall short of the glory of God" (Romans 3:23). It's only through the redemption offered by Jesus Christ that anyone can be made righteous before God. As Paul explained in Romans 2, even though the Jews had the law, none of them followed it well enough to earn their salvation. And in Romans 1, he made the case that the Gentiles (all non-Jews) stood equally condemned.

The Gentiles didn't have the law, Paul said, but they knew God through his creation. Paul wrote that "what may be known about God is plain to them, because God has made it plain to them. For since the creation of the world God's invisible qualities—his eternal power and divine nature—have been clearly seen, being understood from what has been made, so that people are without excuse" (Romans 1:19–20).

Since God had shown himself through creation, even those who lacked written revelation were without excuse. The decisive factor, Paul implied, was whether Gentiles had allowed God's self-revelation to shape their thoughts and actions, or whether they had instead suppressed the truth of God. Their wickedness would be one indication that they had denied God's revealed truth (see Romans 1:18). And the consequences of suppressing that truth were grim. As Paul wrote, "For although they knew God, they neither glorified him as God nor gave thanks to him, but their thinking became futile and their foolish hearts were darkened" (Romans 1:21).

Turning away from God, the Gentiles worshiped idols instead. They "exchanged the glory of the immortal God for images made to look like a mortal human being and birds and animals and reptiles" (Romans 1:23).

How did God respond? He let them go, allowing them to experience the consequences of life without him. "Therefore," Romans 1:24–25 says, "God gave them over in the sinful desires of their hearts to sexual impurity for the degrading of their bodies with one another. They exchanged the truth about God for a lie, and worshiped and served created things rather than the Creator—who is forever praised. Amen."

It was for that reason—their idolatry—that God "gave them over to shameful lusts," as we saw in Romans 1:26–27. They exchanged the truth about God for a lie, so God gave them over to a parallel, sexual exchange: "Even their women exchanged natural relations for unnatural ones," and the men "abandoned natural relations with women and were inflamed with lust for one another."

Paul closed the chapter by describing the final stage of the Gentiles' moral degeneration—and the outcome was bleak. "Furthermore, just as they did not think it worthwhile to retain the knowledge of God, so God gave them over to a depraved mind, so that they do what ought not to be done" (verse 28). Paul listed twenty-one different vices they engaged in—envy, murder, deceit, gossip, slander, hating God, arrogance, faithlessness, and heartlessness, to name a few. He ended by saying, "Although they know God's righteous decree that those who do such things deserve death, they not only continue to do these very things but also approve of those who practice them" (verse 32).

If someone you love follows Christ but is in a same-sex relationship, he or she would appear to have been swept up by Paul and deposited in the dustbin of condemnation. Paul seems to declare them lost—along with God haters, murderers, the faithless, and the heartless—and deserving of death.

Now, it's true that Paul immediately pivoted in Romans 2 to condemn the hypocritical self-righteousness of those who pass judgment even on the degenerate Gentiles. After all, Paul noted, we all fall short of God's righteousness. But his words in Romans 1 have long been read as a rejection of all same-sex relationships. What we need to ask is: is that a faithful application of the text today?

THE REASON FOR PAUL'S CONDEMNATION

Paul's description of same-sex behavior in this passage is indisputably negative. But he also explicitly described the behavior he condemned as lustful. He made no mention of love, fidelity, monogamy, or commitment. So how should we understand Paul's words? Do they apply to all same-sex relationships? Or only to lustful, fleeting ones?

How we answer those questions has profound implications for our conversation in this book. If there's a substantial difference between the type of behavior Paul condemned and the intimate, committed relationships of gay Christians, then he has *not* relegated our gay friends and loved ones to the proverbial dustbin. But if his moral objection in

Romans 1 was to the anatomical sameness of the partners, not primarily to lustfulness, then that rationale would extend to all same-sex relationships.

Focusing on the reasoning behind biblical statements is not a new approach. Christians of all stripes ask not only *what*, but *why* when we study Scripture. For instance, there never has been a serious debate about whether the New Testament writers tell slaves to submit to their masters. They clearly do. (Examples include Titus 2:9–10; 1 Timothy 6:1–2; Colossians 3:22–25; Ephesians 6:5–9; and 1 Peter 2:18–25.)

The question we ask today is not *what* the New Testament writers' instructions to slaves were, but *why* the writers gave the instructions they did.[3] For instance, Titus 2:10 offers a specific rationale for why slaves should submit to their masters: "So that in every way they will make the teaching about God our Savior attractive." The principle here is advancing the gospel, and slaves' submission is described as the most effective way they can accomplish this goal within their culture. But while our need to spread the gospel hasn't changed, the specific ways we pursue this goal have changed. Certainly, it would be difficult to find any Christians today who would give the same advice we find in Titus to an escaped slave in India.[4]

Another example of how Christians distinguish between specific practices and the principles that underlie them is Paul's frequent instructions to Christians to "greet one another with a holy kiss." While platonic kisses were a customary form of greeting in the ancient Mediterranean, they don't carry the same meaning today in most of the West. Most modern Christians seek to live out the principle of Paul's commands—giving a warm welcome—but in different ways.[5]

When it comes to same-sex relationships, we need to discern *why* Paul wrote what he did—the principle behind his statements. Once we answer that question, we can determine how to apply his words most faithfully today. Many non-affirming Christians believe Paul condemned same-sex behavior in Romans 1 because same-sex unions violate God's "natural" intention of anatomical complementarity between men and women. As New Testament professor William Webb has written, "The creative architecture of male and female sexuality with its part-and-counterpart configuration argues against same-sex relationships."[6] If Webb is right that human anatomy forms the basis of Paul's judgment, then that judgment would extend even to loving, committed same-sex couples. But is that why Paul said what he did in Romans 1?

To answer that question, we'll look at the meanings of the words *natural* and *unnatural* in ancient writings, as well as the broader cultural context of Paul's statements. To start, let's consider an influential argument that some affirming Christians have made in recent years for how we should understand the words *natural* and *unnatural*. I don't fully agree with this argument, as it glosses over some important issues. But it does help to point us in the right direction, which is why I want to share it with you now.

Straight People Acting Like Gay People?

Several decades ago, historian John Boswell contended that Paul condemned only same-sex behavior that was practiced by heterosexual people. According to Boswell's reading, Paul denounced same-sex behavior because it was unnatural to the individuals engaging in it—that is to say, it went against their own heterosexual natures. But, Boswell suggested, Paul might have taken a different view of same-sex behavior practiced by those who were naturally attracted to those of the same sex.[7]

There is something compelling about this view. In Romans 1, Paul described people who "exchange" or "abandon" opposite-sex for same-sex relations. So perhaps it's reasonable to think that Paul was condemning, as Boswell argued, "homosexual acts committed by apparently heterosexual persons."[8]

The argument makes sense to that point. But there's a problem. As we saw in chapter 2, the concept of same-sex orientation didn't exist in the ancient world. But this did *not* mean everyone was presumed to be heterosexual. In general, people were thought to be capable of both opposite-sex *and* same-sex attraction. Consequently, there's no reason Paul would have viewed same-sex behavior as contrary to the innate inclinations of many.

His description of same-sex desire in Romans 1:24–27 sounds as if he understood the desire to be innate. In verse 24, he wrote that "God gave them over in the sinful desires of their hearts to sexual impurity." That doesn't sound like the desires were foreign to them. His language in verse 26 is similar, speaking of how God "gave them over to shameful lusts." In both cases, Paul seems to be describing latent desires that were being expressed, not brand-new ones.

And after all, what difference would it make if a desire were innate or not? We all have innate impulses to do countless things we shouldn't do. Many of the vices Paul himself listed in verses 29–31 come to us quite "naturally"—gossip, slander, and boasting, to name a few. So I don't think it's consistent to say that Paul rejected same-sex behavior only when it didn't come naturally to the people involved.

Reaching an Understanding

That said, Boswell's argument does highlight an important distinction between Paul's discussion of same-sex behavior and our conversation about gay Christians. Paul's words indicate not only that the people he described exchanged opposite-sex for same-sex relations, but also that they were *capable* of heterosexual attraction. This understanding would match the expectations of ancient societies, and it would also fit with the rest of the Romans passage.

With each vice Paul listed in Romans 1:18–32, humans are capable of making the opposite, virtuous choice. Instead of worshiping idols, we can choose to worship God. Rather than succumbing to greed, we can choose to give generously. Instead of hating, we can choose to love. For Paul, same-sex relations fit into that same pattern: Rather than following same-sex attractions, we can follow opposite-sex attractions. A second-century Greek dialogue discouraging same-sex behavior reflected that understanding, saying, "If each man were established on the rules which Providence ordained for us, we would be satisfied with intercourse with women and life would be free from every reproach."[9] In other words, men who engage in same-sex behavior *could* be satisfied with sex with women, but their rampant lust leads them beyond it.

As the failure of the modern "ex-gay" movement has shown, however, that isn't the case for gay people. Gay people cannot choose to follow opposite-sex attractions, because they have no opposite-sex attractions to follow—nor can they manufacture them. So, some might ask, does that mean Paul was wrong and the Bible is in error?

No. We have to remember: what Paul was describing is *fundamentally different from what we are discussing.*

A CONDEMNATION OF EXCESS PASSION

As we saw in chapter 2, same-sex relations in the first century were not thought to be the expression of an exclusive sexual orientation. They were widely understood to be the product of excessive sexual desire in general. This understanding, I want to stress, cannot be reduced to a mere misconception. It was a reflection of widespread cultural practices that differ greatly from modern ones.

Remember, the most common forms of same-sex behavior in the Greco-Roman world were pederasty, prostitution, and sex between masters and their slaves. The majority of men who indulged in those practices also engaged in heterosexual behavior, often during the same times in their lives. That isn't to say that *no one* pursued only same-sex relationships, or that no same-sex unions were marked by long-term commitment and love. But such examples were rare enough that the overwhelming majority of visible same-sex behavior fit easily into a paradigm of excess.

In Philo's discussion of Sodom, which we read in chapter 4, we saw this same understanding of same-sex relations as evidence of excess. And when Plato advocated outlawing male same-sex relations in ancient Greece, he explained that his proposal would help curb "erotic frenzy and madness, all forms of adultery, and all immoderate consumption of food and drink." He also noted that a ban on male same-sex relations would have a positive impact on the "loving bond between husbands and their wives," indicating that he assumed men who engaged in same-sex behavior would also be married to women.[10]

In a society that prized moderation as a prime virtue, the excessive nature of same-sex behavior as it was widely practiced revealed a lack of self-control. Dio Chrysostom expressed it well in a first-century speech:

> The man whose appetite is insatiate in such things [referring to sex with women], when he finds there is no scarcity, no resistance, in this field, will have contempt for the easy conquest and scorn for a woman's love, as a thing too readily

given—in fact, too utterly feminine—and will turn his assault against the male quarters, eager to befoul the youth who will very soon be magistrates and judges and generals, believing that in them he will find a kind of pleasure difficult and hard to procure.[11]

In this light, same-sex relations were not objectionable because the partners shared the same anatomy. Dio and others saw them as wrong instead because they stemmed from hedonistic self-indulgence. As he explained in a revealing analogy immediately following the above quote, "His state is like that of men who are addicted to drinking and wine-bibbing, who after long and steady drinking of unmixed wine, often lose their taste for it and create an artificial thirst by the stimulus of sweatings, salted foods, and condiments."[12]

Some people, Dio said, are so insatiable that ordinary pleasures no longer satisfy them. They try to intensify their desires through new, exotic modes of self-gratification. With thirst, that means finding a new stimulus through steam baths and salty foods. With sex, it means abandoning the "easy conquest" of women for rarer, more challenging sex with males. Both Dio and Paul saw everyone as having the same basic appetite for sex. In moderation, that appetite manifested itself in heterosexual desire and behavior. But in excess, it led to same-sex desire and behavior.

That is the cultural context in which Paul's original audience would have read Romans 1:26–27. Paul wasn't condemning the expression of a same-sex orientation as opposed to the expression of an opposite-sex orientation. He was condemning *excess* as opposed to *moderation*.

A fourth-century commentary on the passage by John Chrysostom shows how early Christians interpreted Paul's words:

No one can say that it was by being prevented from legitimate intercourse that they came to this pass or that it was from having no means to fulfill their desire that they were driven into this monstrous insanity.... Notice how deliberately Paul measures his words. For he does not say that they were enamored of one another but that they were consumed by lust for one another! You see that the whole of desire comes from an excess which cannot contain itself within its proper limits.[13]

In Paul's day, same-sex relations were a potent symbol of sexual excess. They offered an effective illustration of Paul's argument: We lose control when we are left to our own devices. We have no moral anchor without God, so chaos and confusion are a typical result when we abandon him.

While that principle remains true today, the specific example Paul drew from his culture doesn't carry the same resonance for us. That isn't because Paul was wrong—he wasn't addressing what we think of today as homosexuality. The context in which Paul discussed same-sex relations differs so much from our own that it can't reasonably be called the same issue.

Same-sex behavior condemned as excess doesn't translate to homosexuality condemned as an orientation—or as a loving expression of that orientation. Given the cultural status of same-sex behavior in the ancient world, it's not surprising that Paul condemned it. He opposed all forms of lust—sexual desire indulged to the excessive height of same-sex behavior would have been no exception.

Where does this leave gay Christians who seek committed relationships? They don't pursue same-sex relationships because they've grown tired of heterosexuality and are seeking a new outlet for their insatiable lusts. They pursue same-sex unions for the same reasons straight Christians pursue opposite-sex unions. They desire intimacy, companionship, and long-term commitment.

THE QUESTION OF NATURE

All right, you may be thinking, same-sex relations for Paul represented excessive passion and lust. But Paul also called them "unnatural." Wouldn't that designation apply to all same-sex unions, no matter the motivation for pursuing them?

The idea that same-sex relationships are "unnatural" has had a tremendous and enduring influence in our society. For many non-affirming Christians, Paul's use of this word in Romans 1 is *the* reason they remain opposed to same-sex relationships even in light of new information about sexual orientation.

As conservative political activist Bryan Fischer has remarked, "Same-sex behavior is unnatural, it is against the order of nature.... You just look at the plumbing and you can tell that, what body parts are designed for what use, and you can see right away that this is contrary to nature."[14] Chuck Colson made a similar case, endorsing a pastor's statement that same-sex behavior is "not normal." "Stand up a naked man and a naked woman and look at them and you'll see what's normal," the pastor said. "That's pretty much what Paul is saying in Romans 1," Colson added.[15]

But *is* that what Paul was saying? It's true that many ancient writers used the terms *natural* and *unnatural* in a broad sense, and the context of their statements indicates that they were referring to something larger than individual disposition. But when we look at their writings more closely, we see that their primary concern wasn't with the shape and fit of human anatomy—with "the plumbing," so to speak. Their primary concern was rooted in a dynamic we saw in chapter 5 (one that I argued is not normative for Christians): patriarchy.

Customary and Uncustomary Gender Roles

In the ancient world, if a man took the active role in sex, his behavior generally was deemed to be "natural." But if he took the passive role, he was derided for engaging in "unnatural" sex. The opposite was true for women: sexual passivity was termed "natural," while sexual dominance was "unnatural."

Same-sex relations challenged those beliefs about nature and sex by putting a male in the passive role or a female in the active role. This inversion of accepted gender roles, combined with the non-procreative character of same-sex unions, is why ancient writers called same-sex behavior "unnatural."

Plato, who lived and wrote more than four hundred years before Paul, is a leading example. In his dialogue *Laws,* Plato contrasted "natural" sex between men and women "for the purpose of procreation" with "unnatural" sex between same-sex partners.[16] In another dialogue, Plato emphasized the problem of gender-role transgressions in same-sex unions. As Plutarch would later quote him, same-sex behavior is shameful because it involves "weakness and effeminacy on the part of those who, contrary to nature, allow themselves in Plato's words 'to be covered and mounted like cattle.'"[17]

The first-century Jewish writer Josephus labeled procreative heterosexual sex "natural" and same-sex behavior "unnatural." He also argued that women are "inferior in every respect" to men.[18] Philo, after condemning men who "[mount] males without respect for the sex nature which the active partner shares with the passive," accused them of spreading a "female disease."[19]

Philo's view of women as inferior was the main reason he objected to same-sex behavior. It required "those who [are] by nature men to submit to play the part of women."[20] Applying the same principle to women, the first-century Jewish text *Sentences of Pseudo-Phocylides* warned females not to "imitate in any way the sexual role of men."[21] A third-century Greek text also taught that "neither should the female be masculinized contrary to nature nor too should the male be softened in an improper manner."[22]

These texts show us how the terms *natural* and *unnatural* were used in ancient writings. They were not synonyms for *straight* and *gay*. They were boundary markers between what did and didn't conform to customary gender roles in a patriarchal context. In fact, some interpreters argue that Romans 1:26 doesn't even refer to female same-sex relations, but to heterosexual sex that was considered "unnatural" because a woman was in the dominant position.[23]

In societies that viewed women as inferior, sexual relationships between equal-status partners could not be accepted. Same-sex unions in particular disrupted a social order that required a strict hierarchy between the sexes. We see that hierarchy reflected in Romans 1 by the use of the phrase "their women" in verse 26, which points to the subordinate role of women in ancient times.[24] And in Jewish and Christian circles, as we saw in the last chapter, men who penetrated other males were also condemned, as they were seen as degrading their passive partner's masculine honor.

What does that cultural background mean for us today? Not all Christians support equal roles for men and women in the church, but none of us would affirm Josephus's statement that women are "inferior in every respect" to men. Nor would we describe femininity as a "disease," as Philo did. And we certainly wouldn't call females "deformed males," as Aristotle did. But such views of women shaped the ancient categories of "natural" and "unnatural" sex that are used in Romans 1.

That observation, of course, raises a similar question to the one we asked in the last chapter: Does that mean Paul was sexist and that modern Christians should simply leave behind some of his outdated views?

But once again, framing the question in such simplistic terms misses the bigger picture. Paul, as we saw in chapter 5, may not have endorsed fully equal roles for men and women, but his views were remarkably egalitarian within his cultural context. As one example, Paul said in 1 Corinthians 7:4, "The wife does not have authority over her own body but yields it to her husband. In the same way, the husband does not have authority over his own body but yields it to his wife." That statement of mutual authority, though followed by one of hierarchy four chapters later (1 Corinthians 11:3–10), notably contrasts with the misogynistic attitudes of the day.

Tarring Paul as sexist is inaccurate. But Paul didn't coin the terms "natural" and "unnatural" as labels for sexual behavior. As we've seen, those labels preceded him by centuries in secular writings. By the time he wrote Romans in the first century, Paul could invoke those terms as a shorthand reference due to their well-established usage. But the terms don't appear in the Old Testament, undermining the idea that Paul used them to make a theological statement about gender complementarity.

It's true, though, that some aspects of the language in Romans 1 do recall language in Genesis 1, as Robert Gagnon and others have noted. Words like "creation" and "Creator," "females" and "males," and "image" and "likeness," among others, appear in both passages. According to Gagnon, "These echoes establish that Paul's main problem with homosexual practice was that it was a violation of God's will for male-female pairing established in creation."[25]

But as Gagnon himself has written, "For Paul all human rebellions are in one way or another rebellions against God's will for humankind set in motion at creation."[26] Any lustful sex would violate God's intention at creation, so the lustful same-sex behavior Paul condemned in Romans 1 would go against God's intention at creation by default. The more pertinent question is whether *all* same-sex relationships would violate the creation order—in other words, whether the violation related to creation runs deeper than lustfulness that leads people to go beyond the male-female union. Gagnon contends that the core problem is the violation of anatomical complementarity, but his argument is highly speculative.[27]

Whatever other "echoes" of Genesis 1 exist in Romans 1, the words "natural" and "unnatural" don't appear in Genesis 1. And as we've seen above, the established use of those terms was related to culture-determined gender roles. Those gender roles, of course, have changed. The words were not primarily related to biology-determined anatomy, which has not changed.

NATURE, HONOR, AND SHAME

An understanding of the labels "natural" and "unnatural" as referring to cultural conventions is further supported by other uses of the Greek words that reflect ancient customs. The *Theological Dictionary of the New Testament* explains that, in ancient Greek, *normal* and *abnormal* were often synonymous with *natural* and *unnatural*.[28]

This is why the Greek writer Euripides could write about an illness that caused "unnatural pain." The pain arose from natural processes, but Euripides called it unnatural because it was unusually intense.[29] The Greek historian Polybius, too, equated things that are unnatural with those that are "beyond the ordinary conceptions of mankind."[30] Plutarch said all diseases and fevers were unnatural, as was courage in women.[31] Seneca and Cicero extended the list even further, including hot baths, banquets held after sunset, drinking on an empty stomach, and walking backward. These were all viewed by some authors as offenses against "nature."[32]

Paul himself used the word "nature" to refer to what we understand as "custom." In 1 Corinthians 11:13–15, after instructing women to pray with their heads covered, Paul wrote, "Judge for yourselves: Is it proper for a woman to pray to God with her head uncovered? Does not the very *nature* of things teach you that if a man has long hair, it is a *disgrace* to him, but that if a woman has long hair, it is her glory?"

The words "nature" and "disgrace" here are the same words Paul used when describing same-sex behavior in Romans 1:26–27. But most Christians today don't read 1 Corinthians 11 as a teaching about God's design for human hairstyles and head coverings. We generally interpret Paul as referring to the customary practices of his day and the societal shame caused by deviating from them. The way many Christians read this passage is along these lines: "Don't the customs of our society teach us that it's considered shameful for a man to have long hair, but honorable for a woman?"

This interpretation helps us reconcile 1 Corinthians 11 with the Old Testament's statements about hair length. Numbers 6:5 says that men who take the Nazirite vow "must let their hair grow long" in order to set themselves apart for the Lord. Second Samuel 14:26 praises Absalom's abundant hair, and 2 Kings 2:23 recounts how Elisha was taunted for his baldness.

So how can it always be disgraceful for a man to have long hair? We can't reach that conclusion in light of the Old Testament's positive statements about long hair in men. But we do have writings from Paul's day associating long, uncovered hair in women with sexual suggestiveness, which helps explain Paul's insistence in 1 Corinthians 11:5–6 that women should wear head coverings.[33]

Scholars often describe the Mediterranean societies of Paul's day as "honor-shame cultures."[34] Honor and shame functioned as a social currency. But what was regarded as honorable or shameful in one culture could vary in another. As we just saw, long hair was often honorable for men in Old Testament times, but norms had changed by the time of the New Testament.

A focus on honor and shame can help us confirm the reasons for Paul's negative statements about same-sex behavior. As New Testament professor James Brownson has written, "What is degrading and shameless about the behavior described in Romans 1:24–27 is that it is driven by excessive, self-seeking lust, that it knows no boundaries or restraints, and that it violates established gender roles of that time and culture, understood in terms of masculine rationality and honor."[35]

The key point to note in that analysis, which matches what we've reviewed in this chapter, is that *none of those reasons extends to the loving, committed relationships of gay Christians today.* The main argument for why Romans 1 should extend to gay Christians—anatomical complementarity—is not supported by the text itself.[36]

Even though Romans 1:18–32 cannot be understood as a narrative about "sameness" and difference, it *can* be understood as a narrative about honor and shame. The English Standard Version translates Romans 1:21 as "Although they knew God, they did not *honor* him as God." The idol worshipers failed to give God the honor he was due, so in a stroke of poetic justice, God allowed them to dishonor themselves as the penalty for their idolatrous error. In the same way, God gave them over to all the vices in verses 28–32, which compounded their shame.[37]

This focus on honor and shame helps explain the statement in Romans 1:27 that those engaging in same-sex excesses "received in themselves the due penalty for their error." Their shameful behavior *was* the penalty.[38] Male passivity, female dominance, and a total lack of self-control made same-sex behavior both the height of sexual excess and the pinnacle of dishonor for many conservative moralists in Paul's day. These factors also made same-sex relations a particularly apt illustration for Paul as he described a consequence of failing to honor God: we ourselves are given over to dishonor.

Using a Good Thing Well

In this chapter, we've considered the key passage of this debate—a passage that has long been interpreted as God's rejection of all same-sex relationships. We've found that, while Paul's words are certainly negative, they appear in a context that differs greatly from the debate taking place within the church today.

For Paul, same-sex desire did not characterize a small minority of people who were subject to special classification—and condemnation—on that basis. Rather, it represented an innate potential for excess within *all* of fallen humanity. When that potential was acted upon, it became "unnatural" in the sense that it subverted conventional, patriarchal gender norms.

As the fifth-century Christian bishop Julian of Eclanum explained it, Paul was contrasting those who make a "right use" of sexual desire with those "abandoned persons [who] indulge" in the "excess of it." For Julian, the moral of the Romans 1 passage was this: "He who observes moderation in natural [desire] uses a good thing well; but he who does not observe moderation abuses a good thing."[39]

From the church's early centuries through the nineteenth century, commentators consistently identified the moral problem in Romans 1:26–27 as "unbridled passions," not the expression of a same-sex orientation.[40] Furthermore, no biblical interpreter prior to the twentieth century even hinted that Paul's statements were intended to consign a whole group of people to lifelong celibacy.

If we are truly to be faithful to the meaning of Scripture, we must rethink how we are interpreting and applying this passage today. Once we do, stories like those of Bobby Griffith—who took his life because he believed this verse and others to condemn him—will not continue to maim the body of Christ.

Will Gay People Inherit the Kingdom of God?

I am far from the only gay Christian who has heard the claim that gay people will not inherit the kingdom of God. That message is plastered on protest signs at gay-pride parades. It's shouted by roaming street preachers at busy intersections and on college campuses. The result is that, for many lesbian, gay, bisexual, and transgender people, all they've heard about the kingdom of God is that they won't be in it.

So far, we've focused on big-picture issues such as tradition, patriarchy, passion, and nature. But in this chapter, we'll go to the heart of a message that damages the witness of Christians and gives LGBT people a damaged perception of God. We'll explore the original meanings of terms that are used to tell gay people they'll be excluded from God's kingdom.

And it involves just two words.

How we understand these words has a very real impact on millions of people, so an in-depth study is worth our time. Since I am not a linguist, and you most likely don't read ancient Greek, we will use plenty of supporting examples to assist us.

THE TWO WORDS IN QUESTION

The crucial words that we'll examine appear in Paul's first letter to the church in Corinth. As it's translated in the King James Version of the Bible, Paul wrote:

> Know ye not that the unrighteous shall not inherit the king-dom of God? Be not deceived: neither fornicators, nor idolaters, nor adulterers, nor effeminate [*malakoi*], nor abusers of themselves with mankind [*arsenokoitai*], nor thieves, nor covetous, nor drunkards, nor revilers, nor extortioners, shall inherit the kingdom of God. (1 Corinthians 6:9–10)

Here, Paul listed ten types of people whose unrighteous conduct prevents them from inheriting God's kingdom. (A similar list in Ephesians 5:3–5 uses even more sweeping language, saying that no one who is "immoral, impure or greedy…has any inheritance in the kingdom of Christ and of God.")

In our time, the debate over gay Christians centers on the question of whether same-sex relationships are sinful. So two of the terms used in this passage are important for our discussion. *Malakoi* here is translated "effeminate," and *arsenokoitai* is translated "abusers of themselves with mankind." In recent years, many Bible translators have chosen to render one or both of these terms as references to gay people or gay relationships.

For example, the English Standard Version translates the terms as "men who practice homosexuality." The New American Standard Bible says "homosexuals." The New Living Translation says "those who…are male prostitutes, or practice homosexuality." Given the prevalence and impact of such translations today, let's look at the arguments and ideas that have influenced them.

THE GREEK WORD *MALAKOI* ("EFFEMINATE")

Malakos (the singular of *malakoi*) was a commonly used term in ancient Greek. It literally means "soft," and it appears elsewhere in the New Testament to describe fine clothing (see Matthew 11:8).

In a moral context, the term was used to describe a lack of self-control, weakness, laziness, or cowardice. Based on the writings we reviewed earlier, I doubt you'll be surprised to learn that the word was an all-purpose insult for anything considered to be feminine. That's why it was long translated as "effeminate" rather than "soft."[1]

Women, remember, were thought to lack control over their appetites and emotions, whereas men—or at least "real" men—were seen as models of temperance and reason. Cicero bluntly expressed prevailing views of femininity when he gave this advice: "Everything comes down to this: that you rule yourself.... [Do not] do anything in a base, timid, ignoble, slavelike, or womanish way."[2] Seneca, too, explained, "If I must suffer illness, it will be my wish to do nothing out of control, nothing effeminately."[3]

For writers of Paul's day, to be effeminate was to be weak and out of control. That shortcoming wasn't necessarily related to sexual behavior, so most activities that were derided as being "soft" were not sexual. Things such as gambling, greed, and vanity were called "soft," as were drunkenness and a fondness for fine foods.[4] A number of ancient writers used the term *malakoi* to condemn men for their laziness, cowardice, and extravagance.[5]

Weakness and excess could involve sexual conduct, of course. Some men who engaged in same-sex behavior were indeed mocked as *mala-koi*—specifically, men who willingly submitted to penetration. On that basis, many biblical translators in recent decades have translated the term as a condemnation of homosexuality, or at least a condemnation of men who take the passive role in same-sex relations.

But there are problems with that interpretation. First, as I mentioned, most uses of the word *malakos* were not related to sexual behavior. But even if we look only at the word's sexual uses, "passive same-sex behavior" still is not the word's most likely meaning. The word *malakos* was actually more frequently applied to men who succumbed to the charms of *women*.

For those of us living in societies that generally equate any same-sex attraction in males with effeminacy, that idea can seem puzzling. From our standpoint, the more aggressively a man pursues a woman, the more masculine he seems. And if he's at all interested in other men, he's expected to be effeminate. But ancient societies didn't share these expectations, largely because they didn't distinguish between heterosexuality and homosexuality as sexual orientations in the first place. As I noted in earlier chapters, their main concern was whether people conformed to expected gender roles.

- Men were strong. Women were weak, or "softies."
- Men were courageous. Women were cowardly.
- Men were dominant. Women were submissive.
- Men were models of restraint. Women lacked self-control.

If a man did anything that was typically associated with women, he opened himself to the charge of being a *malakos*. That could even involve his overzealous pursuit of women, as it could betray his "effeminate" lack of self-control.[6]

Odd as it sounds to us, the concept of an "effeminate womanizer" was commonplace in ancient literature. In a second-century BC Roman comedy, for instance, a male suitor dismisses his rival as a "soft woman-izer who has his hair in ringlets, who lives in the shade, [and] who plays a tambourine."[7] Seneca the Elder, a contemporary of Paul, leveled simi-lar invective at a man consumed by his passions for women. Seneca wrote, "Dripping with foreign perfumes, crippled by his lusts, *walking more softly than a woman in order to please women*—and all the other things that show not judgment but disorder" (emphasis added).[8]

Being "soft" in a sexual sense meant that a man was self-indulgent and enslaved to his passions. He was ruled by someone or something other than himself. In that sense, being passive in same-sex relations *and* falling head over heels in love with a woman both were markers of effeminacy.

A man's falling prey to a woman's charms, in some quarters, could invite even worse censure than sexual passivity with males. After all, men who allowed other men to dominate them were "acting like women," but at least they were still under the control of a *man*. But if a man fell under a woman's thrall, he had succumbed to the definition of weakness.

This perspective, I should note, did not hold true for men who had sex with women but kept control of their emotions in the process. It applied only to men who were seen as excessively doting on women. Even the famed Roman general Pompey was criticized for excessive devotion to his wife. As Plutarch put it, Pompey "weakly succumbed to his passion for his young wife, devoting himself almost exclusively to her...and neglecting affairs of the forum." His behavior inspired mock-ery of him as "the general with no self-control."[9] Likewise, in Plutarch's *Dialogue on Love,* forms of the word *malakos* are applied to men who love women.[10]

So even the sexual sense of *malakos* doesn't necessarily refer to same-sex behavior. In fact, reading it as a reference to same-sex behavior is a recent trend in biblical interpretation. Most English Bible translations prior to the twentieth century that deviated from the term *effeminate* translated the word as a general injunction against wantonness, not a specific condemnation of same-sex behavior. Note how *malakos* was translated in these Bible versions:

- "weaklinges" (1525, Tyndale New Testament)
- "wantons" (1587, Geneva Bible)
- "debauchers" (1852, James Murdock translation)
- "licentious" (1904, Ernest Malan translation)
- "sensual" (1923, Edgar Goodspeed translation)

New Testament scholar David Fredrickson has argued that *malakoi* in 1 Corinthians 6:9 be translated as "those who lack self-control."[11] Based on the evidence, that translation stands on firmer footing than any interpretation that defines the word as a specific reference to same-sex behavior. As we've seen, *malakoi* doesn't refer to merely a single act. It encompasses an entire disposition toward immoderation.

But even if *malakoi* doesn't usually refer to same-sex relations, there is a second crucial word to contend with. According to some non-affirming Christians, even if *malakoi* on its own is ambiguous, we should understand it as a condemnation of same-sex relations given the word that follows it in 1 Corinthians 6. That word is *arsenokoitai*.

THE GREEK WORD *ARSENOKOITAI*
("ABUSERS OF THEMSELVES WITH MANKIND")

The word *arsenokoitai* (the plural of *arsenokoites*) was used very rarely in ancient Greek writings. In fact, Paul's use of the word in 1 Corinthians 6 is widely considered to be its first use in ancient literature. Afterward, the term appears mostly in lists of vices, which are of limited help in determining its meaning. Unlike *malakoi*, though, the term *arsenokoitai* was understood by Bible translators before the twentieth century to refer to same-sex behavior.

In Greek, *arsen* means "male" and *koites* means "bed," typically with a sexual connotation. Given the meaning of those words, some argue that *arsenokoitai* must mean "men who sleep with other men," encompassing a condemnation of non-celibate gay men.

But the argument breaks down in two key places. First, the component parts of a word don't necessarily tell us what it means. The English word *understand*, for instance, has nothing to do with either "standing" or being "under." If a person learning English as a second language tried to figure out the meaning of *understand* only by considering its component parts, she would be led far astray.

Some non-affirming Christians seek to avoid this difficulty by connecting *arsenokoitai* to the prohibition of male same-sex intercourse found in Leviticus 20:13. In the earliest Greek translation of that verse, the words *arsenos koiten* appear next to one another. So it's possible that Paul coined the term *arsenokoitai* based on his familiarity with the Greek translation of Leviticus 20. If so, he likely *was* using the word to condemn some form of same-sex behavior.

But if this is the case, another possibility crops up. As we saw in chapter 2, the most common forms of same-sex behavior in the ancient world were pederasty, prostitution, and sex between masters and slaves. Pederasty, in fact, was so common that Philo described it simply as the union of "males with males." He rightly expected his readers to grasp his specific reference despite the generic nature of his word choice. Given the prominence of pederasty in the ancient world, Paul may have been taking a similar approach through his use of the word *arsenokoitai*.[12]

So even if the compound *arsenokoitai* did originate from Leviticus, that still wouldn't tell us what it means in 1 Corinthians 6. As New Testament scholar Dale Martin has written, "The only reliable way to define a word is to analyze its use in as many different contexts as possible."[13]

Although *arsenokoites* was used quite rarely in Greek literature after Paul, some of the few uses that have survived indicate it most often referred to economic exploitation, not same-sex behavior. Given how frequently this word is used to condemn the intimate relationships of gay people today, it's important that we gain clarity on its meaning in 1 Corinthians 6. To help, let's look at three uses of the word in ancient writings.

An ancient text known as the *Sibylline Oracles* includes a form of the word *arsenokoites* in a section describing violations of justice. The relevant portion reads: "Do not steal seeds. Whoever takes for himself is accursed to generations of generations, to the scattering of life. Do not *arsenokoitein*, do not betray information, do not murder. Give one who has labored his wage. Do not oppress a poor man."[14]

No other injustice in this section is related to sexual behavior. But the *Sibylline Oracles* does denounce a list of sexual vices later on, and the word *arsenokoites* is noticeably absent from that list. Why would the word not be repeated in that context if it had been understood to describe a primarily sexual offense?

Similarly, a second-century text called the *Acts of John* lists the word *arsenokoites* in the context of economic exploitation and power abuses. This text warns: "And let the murderer know that the punishment he has earned awaits him in double measure after he leaves this (world). So also the poisoner, sorcerer, robber, swindler, and *arsenokoites,* the thief and all of this band." The section ends with a declaration that "eternal misery and torment" await "kings, rulers, tyrants, boasters, and warmongers."[15] The *Acts of John* also lists sexual sins in a separate section, and *arsenokoites* doesn't appear there. As in the first text, the word appears only among vices involving economic injustice and abuses of power.

Another second-century Christian text, a letter called *To Autolychus,* uses the word. Here, it's placed more closely to sexual sins. But the first time this letter uses *arsenokoites,* it separates it from sexual sins by three words condemning thieves, plunderers, and defrauders. The second time the word appears, its placement is more ambiguous, situated between sexual sins and sins of exploitation. That positioning has led Dale Martin to suggest that the term *arsenokoites* may describe "economic exploitation by some sexual means."[16]

We shouldn't be surprised to find that both uses of the word in the New Testament place it between sexual and economic vices. In 1 Corinthians 6, the word appears following references to "sexually immoral" and "adulterers" and before "thieves" and the "greedy." In 1 Timothy 1:10, it appears after "sexually immoral" and before "slave traders" or "menstealers."[17] These contexts support the idea that *arsenokoites* describes some kind of sexual *and* economic exploitation.

So what can we reasonably conclude from these findings? One of the most prominent forms of sexual exploitation in the ancient world was the practice of pederasty. If *arsenokoites* does refer to male same-sex behavior, it's possible that it refers to pederasty.[18] But given the scarcity of the word in ancient literature, the most we can say with confidence is that it may refer to some kind of economic exploitation involving sexual behavior. While that may have included same-sex behavior, it would likely have been exploitative forms of it.

MINOR SHIFT, MAJOR IMPLICATIONS

We've examined these words separately, along with the most likely meaning of each one. Now, let's look at the meaning of the two words as used together. Perhaps Paul's placement of *malakos* and *arsenokoites* next to each other indicates we should understand them as a pair, condemning *both* passive and active forms of same-sex behavior.[19]

That's the case made by many non-affirming Christians, and it helps explain why some modern English Bible translations combine the two words, rendering them as a sweeping condemnation of all "men who have sex with men." But *malakos* and *arsenokoites* were never used as a pair by other ancient writers, so that idea rests on speculation. Other word pairs were in common use to describe both partners in same-sex relations—words such as *erastes* and *eromenos,* or *paiderastes* and *kinaidos.*

But here's the key point to remember: even if Paul *had* intended his words to be a condemnation of both male partners in same-sex relations, the context in which he would have been making that statement would still differ significantly from our context today.

As we have seen, same-sex behavior in the first century was not understood to be the expression of an exclusive sexual orientation. It was understood as excess on the part of those who could easily be content with heterosexual relationships, but who went beyond them in search of more exotic pleasures.[20]

That conceptual difference, I should emphasize, isn't confined to the ancient world. We see it reflected in the history of how the word *arsenokoitai* was translated into English. Most English-language Bible translations over the past five hundred years have connected the term to male same-sex behavior. But until the past century, Bible translators didn't describe same-sex behavior as the expression of a sexual orientation. To give you a sense of what I mean, here's a sampling of how *arsenokoitai* was translated into English from the sixteenth through the nineteenth centuries:

- 1525: "abusars of them selves with the mankynde" (Tyndale New Testament)
- 1587: "buggerers" (Geneva Bible)
- 1729: "the brutal" (Mace New Testament)
- 1755: "sodomites" (Wesley's New Testament)
- 1899: "liers with mankind" (Douay-Rheims American Edition)

"Sodomites" and "buggerers" were labels applied on the basis of acts, not desires. Once a person ceased engaging in "sodomy" or "buggery" (terms that could encompass *all* non-procreative sexual acts), he was no longer considered a sodomite or a buggerer.

But starting in the mid-twentieth century, the translation of *arsenokoitai* shifted in a subtle but significant way. It no longer referred to an act any man might commit, but rather, to a specific type of person whose *sexual orientation* made him uniquely subject to condemnation. Thus, English translations tended more toward "homosexuals" or "homosexual perverts."

- 1946: "homosexuals" (RSV)
- 1958: "pervert" (Phillips)

- 1966: "homosexual perverts" (TEV)
- 1973: "homosexual offenders" (NIV)
- 1987: "practicing homosexuals" (NAB)

As the concept of sexual orientation came to be more widely understood, some Bible versions changed "homosexuals" to "practicing homosexuals" in order to distinguish between an apparently blameless sexual orientation and blameworthy sexual conduct. But this distinction, as we know, was alien to the biblical world. There was no word in ancient Greek, Hebrew, or Latin that corresponds to the English word for "gay," as the concept of an exclusive, permanent same-sex orientation is little more than a century old.

So what are we to make of this minor shift in translation in the mid-twentieth century? It's had significant consequences. It fostered the mistaken belief that Paul was condemning a minority group with a different sexual orientation. Instead, he was likely condemning excessive and exploitative sexual conduct. (Most of the other vices listed in 1 Corinthians 6, it's worth pointing out, can be understood as sins of excess or exploitation: general sexual immorality, adultery, thievery, greed, drunkenness, slander, and swindling.)

But merely changing anachronistic language such as "homosexuals" to "men who have sex with men," as some modern translators have done, is little better. Such sweeping language still obscures the fundamental differences between how Paul understood same-sex relations and the modern understanding of sexual orientation. In so doing, it wrongly attributes to Paul a position on a hot-button issue he never faced: the question of lesbian, gay, bisexual, and transgender people. This misattribution, however subtle the difference in wording, is a tragedy. It's just a few words, but they have separated millions of people from the transformative power of the gospel.

WHERE DOES THIS LEAVE US?

In the first three chapters of this book, we looked at three significant problems with non-affirming beliefs about homosexuality. First, we saw that a categorical rejection of same-sex relationships has been deeply damaging to gay Christians. This isn't the outcome we should expect given Jesus's teaching that good trees will bear good fruit, so it invites us to reconsider the issue.

In chapter 2, we saw that the concept of same-sex orientation didn't exist in the ancient world. Prior to recent generations, same-sex behavior was widely understood to be the product of sexual excess, not the expression of a sexual orientation. The issue we face today—gay Christians and their committed relationships—hasn't been an issue the church has faced in past eras.

But while there is no church tradition on the issue of gay Christians, we saw in chapter 3 that the church has an established tradition affirming that lifelong celibacy should be voluntarily chosen, not mandated. Maintaining a condemnation of same-sex relationships would require us to revise that teaching, which is grounded in the core doctrines of creation, incarnation, and resurrection.

In light of those problems with the traditional interpretation, we embarked on an exploration of the six Scripture passages most often cited in the debate about gay Christians. In each case, we found that the traditional interpretation doesn't envision the committed relationships of gay Christians.

For instance, the Sodom and Gomorrah story describes a threatened same-sex gang rape, a far cry from intimate companionship. Likewise, the prohibitions of male same-sex intercourse in Leviticus 18:22 and 20:13 were grounded in cultural concerns about patriarchal gender roles, not the anatomical complementarity of men and women. Today's debate takes place in a context far removed from the setting of Leviticus and its prohibitions, a law code that has never applied to Christians.

We then investigated Romans 1:26–27, the central text in this debate. While Paul took a negative view of same-sex behavior in that passage, the language and logic of his discussion differ significantly from the issue of gay Christians. Paul viewed same-sex relations as stemming from excessive sexual desire and lust, not as the loving expression of a sexual orientation. Furthermore, his use of the terms "natural" and "unnatural" reflects a concern about customary gender roles in a patriarchal society, not the anatomical "sameness" of same-sex partners.

Finally, we looked at the disputed Greek terms that appear in 1 Corinthians 6:9 and 1 Timothy 1:10. While *malakoi* and *arsenokoitai* could encompass forms of same-sex behavior, the behavior they might describe bears little resemblance to the modern relationships of lesbian, gay, bisexual, and transgender Christians.

The bottom line is this: The Bible doesn't directly address the issue of same-sex *orientation*—or the expression of that orientation. While its six references to same-sex behavior are negative, the concept of same-sex behavior in the Bible is sexual excess, not sexual orientation. What's more, the main reason that non-affirming Christians believe the Bible's statements should apply to all same-sex relationships—men and women's anatomical complementarity—is not mentioned in any of the texts.

I remember sitting across from my dad at our breakfast-room table as he began to absorb those facts for the first time. We discussed the history of the two words in this chapter along with the other passages, and he started to realize that his assumptions about the Bible and homosexuality had been mistaken. Even though Dad has a humble heart, it was still a blow to his pride to imagine that he could've been wrong on such an important issue for his whole life. But it was also a liberating realization. After spending several months walking with me through these Scripture passages, Dad came to see that his faith may not be compromised by embracing a same-sex relationship for me. He was starting to think that he could continue to affirm the full authority of Scripture, and at the same time, affirm me.

Granted, the Bible's silence on committed same-sex relationships doesn't necessarily mean those relationships are blessed. Even if you agree with my analysis so far, you may still wonder: Can loving, committed same-sex unions fulfill the Bible's understanding of marriage?

Let's look at that question in depth.

The Biblical Argument for Marriage Equality

When I was fifteen, Kansas voters cast their ballots on a constitutional amendment to ban same-sex marriage. I asked my dad how he was going to vote, and he told me he supported the ban.

A few months earlier, I would have agreed with him. But some of my friends had been speaking out against the measure, and I thought they might have a point. "Isn't that discrimination against gay people?" I asked my dad.

"Well," he said, "marriage is different."

For many Christians, that sentiment sums it up. While they are willing to be tolerant toward lesbian, gay, bisexual, and transgender people, the idea of granting marriage rights to same-sex couples is a bridge too far. And the idea of blessing same-sex marriages in the church seems entirely out of the question. Christian marriage is holy, an institution ordained by God. It isn't something we can redefine based on personal feelings or shifts in public opinion.

I agree, Christian marriage *is* different. To be honest, I write this chapter with some trepidation. In his book *This Momentary Marriage*, John Piper mentioned that he waited forty years after his wedding day to write a book on the subject, and I think there is real wisdom to that approach.[1] As a young, unmarried believer, I won't venture to offer advice on married life.

Yet I'm in a different situation than most others who write about marriage. Because I am gay, any marriage I might want to enter would involve another man. And many Christians today question whether a relationship between two men can even *be* a marriage. With that in mind, I have invested considerable time and effort into studying the meaning of marriage.

This chapter is not intended to address everything marriage accomplishes or all the ways marriage can bring us closer to God. I'm not in a position to write about those things. My focus is far more basic. Now that many of us recognize that same-sex orientation is both fixed and unchosen, we need to modify one of two Christian teachings: either the voluntary nature of lifelong celibacy or the scope of marriage. The meaning of Christian celibacy as a gift and chosen calling is undermined when we insist that gay Christians remain celibate as a rejection of their sexuality. (We looked at this issue and the related Christian teachings in chapter 3.) But what about the scope of marriage?

Can same-sex marriage fit a Christian basis for marriage? Let's explore the biblical teachings that touch on this issue. Along those lines, we'll seek to answer two questions: What is the meaning of marriage according to the Bible? And, can same-sex unions fulfill that meaning?

MARRIAGE AS A REFLECTION
OF CHRIST AND THE CHURCH

Ephesians 5:21–33 is arguably the most theologically rich passage in the Bible regarding marriage. In this text, the marriage covenant is related to something much larger than itself. According to Ephesians, marriage is intended to model Christ's love for his church. We read:

> Submit to one another out of reverence for Christ.
>
> Wives, submit yourselves to your own husbands as you do to the Lord. For the husband is the head of the wife as Christ is the head of the church, his body, of which he is the Savior. Now as the church submits to Christ, so also wives should submit to their husbands in everything.
>
> Husbands, love your wives, just as Christ loved the church and gave himself up for her to make her holy, cleansing her by the washing with water through the word, and to present her to himself as a radiant church, without stain or wrinkle or any other blemish, but holy and blameless. In this same way, husbands ought to love their wives as their own bodies. He who loves his wife loves himself. After all, no one ever hated their own body, but they feed and care for their body, just as Christ does the church—for we are members of his body. "For this reason a man will leave his father and mother and be united to his wife, and the two will become one flesh." This is a profound mystery—but I am talking about Christ and the church. However, each one of you also must love his wife as he loves himself, and the wife must respect her husband.

Do you see what this passage is saying? It's taking the marriage language of "one flesh" from Genesis 2:24 and pointing us beyond our original understanding of it. There's no mention here of children, in-laws, property transactions, or marriage as the foundation of a stable society. As important as those things are, this text is looking deeper.

Human marriage, Ephesians says, is a "profound mystery" that points to the ultimate relationship: Christ's eternal union with the church. Given that Christ's covenant with us is unbreakable, our marriage bonds should be equally enduring. So the most important aspect of marriage is the covenant the two partners make.

Perhaps the dominant message about marriage in modern society is that it's primarily about being happy, being in love, and being fulfilled. Nearly everyone desires these things, of course. But what happens to the marriage bond if one spouse stops feeling fulfilled? What if one partner falls out of love, or they both do?

For many in our society, the answer seems obvious: The couple should seek a divorce. Why should two people who no longer love each other stay together?

But that is not the Christian message. For Christians, marriage is not just about us. It's also about Christ. If Christ had kept open the option to leave us behind when he grew frustrated with us or felt like we were not living up to his standards, he may have abandoned us long ago. But the story of the gospel is that, although we don't deserve it, God lavishes his sacrificial love upon us anyway.

In marriage, we're called to reflect God's love for us through our self-giving love for our spouse. God's love for us isn't dependent on our day-to-day feelings toward him, on how hard we work to please him, or even on how faithful we are to him. It's grounded in his nature and his covenant. Ephesians 5:1 tells us to be "imitators of God" (NASB). Because God's love is boundless, ours should be as well. That means marriage isn't, at its deepest level, just about our happiness and fulfillment. At its core, marriage is also about displaying the nature and glory of God through the covenant we make—and keep—with our spouse.

How Does This View of Marriage
Apply to Same-Sex Couples?

If the essence of marriage involves a covenant-keeping relationship of mutual self-giving, then two men or two women can fulfill that purpose as well as a man and a woman can. But is lifelong commitment between two adults sufficient for realizing a Christian basis for marriage? Or is there something unique about heterosexual relationships that prevents same-sex couples from truly illustrating Christ's love for the church?

The first response one might make based on Ephesians 5 is that same-sex unions are necessarily excluded from a Christian basis for marriage because Scripture uses only heterosexual language when describing it. But given the widespread association of same-sex behavior with lustful excess in the ancient world, it isn't surprising that the biblical writers didn't contemplate the possibility of same-sex marriage. Our question isn't whether the Bible addresses the modern concepts of sexual orientation and same-sex marriage. We know it doesn't. Instead, our question is: *Can we translate basic biblical principles about marriage to this new situation without losing something essential in the process?* We need to determine, from a biblical standpoint, whether the essence of Christian marriage permits the inclusion of same-sex couples, or whether it necessarily involves the union of a man and a woman.

We know covenant keeping is essential to Christian marriage. But is gender difference between the spouses also essential?

The Call to Procreate

One reason many non-affirming Christians believe gender difference *is* essential to marriage is the obvious one: Only a man and a woman can biologically procreate. In Genesis 1:28, after verse 27 says that God created humanity "male and female," we read: "God blessed them and said to them, 'Be fruitful and increase in number; fill the earth and subdue it.'" Since same-sex couples cannot increase in number through biological procreation, does that prevent their relationships from fulfilling the Bible's basis for marriage?

From a strictly Old Testament perspective, that position has some merit. In Genesis 12–17, God established his covenant with Abraham. He promised to make Abraham "into a great nation" and to bless him with offspring as numerous as the stars in the sky (see Genesis 12:2; 15:5). When God reaffirmed this covenant with Isaac (see Genesis 26) and Jacob (see Genesis 28), he again emphasized his promise of physical offspring.

In the Old Testament, God was understood to extend his covenantal blessings to Israel primarily through biological procreation. The fear of having his name blotted out is why Saul pleaded with David, "Now swear to me by the LORD that you will not kill off my descendants or wipe out my name from my father's family" (1 Samuel 24:21). That fear also explains the reaction of Jephthah's daughter in Judges 11, when she learned she would be sacrificed. She asked her father for two months to weep with her friends. But she didn't ask to weep because she would soon die, but because she would never marry (see Judges 11:37–39). The emphasis on procreation also led to the marginalization of infertile women and eunuchs. Eunuchs were actually barred from entering the assembly of the Lord (see Deuteronomy 23:1).

But the life, death, and resurrection of Jesus ushered in a host of transformative changes, and one of those changes is vital to our conversation here: Biological procreation no longer determines membership in God's kingdom. Spiritual *re*birth through faith in Christ does.[2]

Under the old covenant, one could simply be born into the people of God. But as Jesus explained to Nicodemus, under the new covenant, "no one can see the kingdom of God unless they are born again" (John 3:3). In the words of John Piper, God's people are now "produced not by physical procreation but by spiritual regeneration."[3]

This change in how the kingdom of God is built has had lasting consequences that pertain to our discussion of same-sex marriage.

First, marriage and procreation are no longer seen as the necessary ways of growing God's family.

Second, lifelong celibacy is a valid option for Christians, even though it generally wasn't for the ancient Israelites.

Third, the definition of family has changed for Christians.

Jesus was preaching to a crowd when his mother and brothers showed up, asking to speak with him. He responded by saying, "Who is my mother, and who are my brothers?" Jesus pointed to his disciples and said, "Here are my mother and my brothers. For whoever does the will of my Father in heaven is my brother and sister and mother" (Matthew 12:46–50).

That shift in understanding is reflected when we call one another a "brother in Christ" or a "sister in Christ." Relationships in Christ are more enduring even than bonds between biological family members. Jesus emphasized that the bonds shared by spouses and members of biological families are temporary because they will not exist in eternity.

"The people of this age marry and are given in marriage," Jesus said. "But those who are considered worthy of taking part in the age to come and in the resurrection from the dead will neither marry nor be given in marriage, and they can no longer die; for they are like the angels. They are God's children, since they are children of the resurrection" (Luke 20:34–36).

The New Testament's focus on personal faith rather than procreation has another important consequence: Even a celibate person can become a spiritual parent by bringing others to faith in Christ. Isaiah foreshadowed this development: " 'Sing, barren woman, you who never bore a child; burst into song, shout for joy, you who were never in labor; because more are the children of the desolate woman than of her who has a husband,' says the LORD" (Isaiah 54:1).

So, too, eunuchs now have reason to rejoice. Isaiah quoted God as saying, "To the eunuchs who keep my Sabbaths, who choose what pleases me and hold fast to my covenant—to them I will give within my temple and its walls a memorial and a name better than sons and daughters" (Isaiah 56:4–5). In Christ, that prophecy is fulfilled. The first Gentile convert to the faith was likely none other than an Ethiopian eunuch (see Acts 8:26–39).

Is Procreation a Fixed Standard in Marriage?

You may be wondering: Even if procreation is no longer expected of all God's people, is it not still expected of all married couples? Does sex, in order to be moral, need at least to offer the possibility of reproduction?

In the original creation story, procreation is not presented as the primary purpose of marriage. While Genesis 1:28 does say to "be fruitful and increase in number," Genesis 2 never mentions procreation when describing the first marriage. And despite the significance of procreation in the Old Testament, infertile marriages were not considered illegitimate. The marriages of Abraham and Sarah (see Genesis 18) as well as Elkanah and Hannah (see 1 Samuel 1) were valid even in the long years before they had a child. In the New Testament, too, Jesus may have made one exception to his prohibition of divorce, saying a couple could divorce in the case of infidelity (see Matthew 19:9). But he made no exception for couples who are unable to bear children. In Jesus's understanding of marriage, covenantal commitment is foundational. The ability to bear children is not.[4]

Additional teachings in Scripture support the understanding that procreation is not essential to marriage. The Song of Songs is an ode to the joys of erotic love and intimacy, wholly separate from a concern for procreation. The Song centers on the delights of bodily pleasure, uplifting sexual arousal and satisfaction as good parts of God's creation. Recall, too, that in 1 Corinthians 7, Paul encouraged married couples to have sex "so that Satan will not tempt you because of your lack of self-control" (verse 5). Paul never suggested that sex was only or even primarily for the purpose of procreation.

From a theological perspective, marriage primarily involves a covenant-keeping relationship of mutual self-giving that reflects God's love for us. The evidence we've considered here indicates that marriage is only secondarily—and not necessarily at all—about having biological children. Same-sex couples' inability to procreate does not exclude them from fulfilling the Bible's basis for marriage.

THE MATTER OF GENDER HIERARCHY

While Ephesians 5 doesn't mention married couples having children, it *does* mention—or at least assumes—gender hierarchy. It calls a man the "head" of his wife just as Christ is the head of the church, and wives are told to submit to their husbands in the same way the church submits to Christ. But same-sex couples can't live out that dynamic. So does the hierarchical aspect of marriage as described in Scripture mean marriage must be between a man and a woman?

This question brings us back to the big-picture idea we discussed in chapter 5: Is the Bible's reflection of patriarchy normative for Christians, or is it limited in a way similar to Scripture's accommodation of slavery? We saw before that ancient societies didn't simply uphold differing roles for men and women; they accorded women inferior *value*.

Few, if any, Christians today would endorse the degrading views of women that shaped the world of Leviticus. However, many Christians do hold beliefs about gender relations that could be summed up as "equal value, different roles." That's the kind of hierarchical gender complementarity we looked at in chapter 2. Gender complementarity is often reflected in distinct gender roles in marriage. In that view, husbands act as the leaders and wives as their followers. As long as spouses affirm the equal value of both genders, might we conclude that such an approach to gender relations is consistent with the New Testament vision of relationships free of patriarchy? Let's look into that question.

In his letter to the Galatians, Paul wrote that three types of hierarchies would fade away in Christ. The first two were distinctions between Jew and Gentile and distinctions between slave and free. The third was that of male and female. Paul's main concern at the time was ending the division between Jews and Gentiles, and Galatians 3:28 is focused on our ultimate status in Christ, not our present status in society.[5]

But in the Sermon on the Mount, Jesus tells us to pray that God's kingdom will come "on earth as it is in heaven" (Matthew 6:10). In opposing slavery, Christians in the nineteenth century took that message to heart. Since there won't be a distinction in God's kingdom of slave and free, Christians decided to abolish the inhumane institution of slavery in the West.

But what does that have to do with the requirements of marriage?

Just this: Christians did not work for change so that slaves would be regarded as having equal value while maintaining a subordinate status and role in society. They chose to abolish the subordinate status altogether. While slavery remains a tragic reality in much of the world, the church now uniformly opposes it.

Given that Paul in Galatians connected the issues of slavery and gender hierarchy, we should as well. The New Testament explicitly links the submission of slaves to the submission of wives. First Peter 3:1 begins, "Wives, in the same way [that slaves are to submit to their masters] submit yourselves to your own husbands..." The comparison comes from the instructions given in 1 Peter 2:18–25. Peter told wives to submit to their husbands *in the same way* slaves were instructed to submit to masters.

We see a similar parallel in the words of Ephesians 5 and 6. Wives are told to submit to their husbands in Ephesians 5, and in chapter 6, slaves are instructed to submit to their masters, "just as you would obey Christ" (Ephesians 6:5).

Yet both hierarchies will fade away in Christ, and Jesus calls us to make that a reality now. Scripture lays the groundwork for a redemptive reordering of gender relations in God's kingdom, so gender hierarchy can't be said to be essential to marriage. Even if, when a man and a woman marry, they don't have a hierarchical relationship, no one claims their marriage is invalid on that basis. Acceptance of these marriages indicates that, even with opposite-sex spouses, gender hierarchy isn't part of the essence of Christian marriage. In keeping with the focus of Ephesians 5, the essence of Christian marriage involves keeping covenant with one's spouse in a relationship of mutual self-giving. That picture doesn't exclude same-sex couples.

THE LANGUAGE OF "ONE FLESH"

Before we draw a final conclusion, we need to take into account the second type of gender complementarity, which I've referred to as anatomical complementarity. Ephesians 5 quotes Genesis 2:24, which describes how "a man leaves his father and mother and is united to his wife, and they become one flesh." Some interpreters argue that the sexual aspect of marriage is not merely a union between two partners, but a *re*union of two particular—and anatomically distinct—bodies that originally came from the same flesh. Because same-sex couples share the same anatomy, this argument continues, they cannot become "one flesh" in the biblical sense.[6]

But as New Testament scholar James Brownson explained in his book *Bible, Gender, Sexuality,* this interpretation oversexualizes the phrase "one flesh." In the Bible, the term "flesh" is used metaphorically to describe ties of kinship. Genesis 29:14 recounts how Laban, upon learning that Jacob was his relative, exclaimed, "Surely you are my bone and my flesh!" (NRSV). Likewise, in 2 Samuel 19:12, David told the elders of Judah, "You are my brothers; you are my bone and my flesh" (ESV).[7] So Genesis 2:23–24, when read in light of Scripture's other uses of the term "flesh," isn't focusing on Adam and Eve's anatomical difference. Its focus instead is on their basic commonality as two people forming a new kinship bond.

The phrase "one flesh" in Genesis 2:24 connotes sexual union as well. As Tim Keller has written, "The word 'united'...means 'to make a binding covenant or contract.' This covenant brings every aspect of two persons' lives together.... To call the marriage 'one flesh,' then, means that sex is understood as both a sign of that personal, legal union and a means to accomplish it."[8] But ultimately, the phrase doesn't depend on a particular sexual act, but on the deep, relational connection that sex can create. As Brownson has written, the "one-flesh" language "points beyond the physical act to the relational connections and intimacy that undergird and surround it."[9] Sexual mechanics for two men or two women vary from what transpires between a man and a woman, but the strength of the resulting bond can be the same.

It's precisely the strength of that bond that underlies the Bible's restriction of sex to marriage. As the greatest form of bodily self-giving, sex should be combined with the greatest form of emotional self-giving: a lifelong commitment to a single partner.[10]

Paul reflected this view when he used the phrase "one flesh" in 1 Corinthians 6:12–20. He rejected the belief of some of the Corinthians that how they used their bodies didn't matter. God won't destroy the body, Paul reminded them. God will resurrect it, just as he did for Christ.

Paul explained that our bodies "are members of Christ himself," so to "take the members of Christ and unite them with a prostitute" is out of the question (verse 15). Paul then used the phrase "one flesh" to clarify his point. "Do you not know that he who unites himself with a prostitute is one with her in body? For it is said, 'The two will become one flesh'" (verse 16).

Becoming "one flesh" encompasses much more than the act of sex. It includes the entire covenantal context in which God intends for sex to take place. Having sex with a prostitute was particularly galling to Paul because it united two bodies without also uniting their lives. It was thus a hollow distortion of the Bible's grand vision for "one-flesh" unions.

CAN SAME-SEX COUPLES
BECOME "ONE FLESH"?

The Bible's language of "one-flesh" unions, which does seem to be part of marriage's essence, rules out sexual promiscuity. But the meaning of the phrase doesn't require gender difference.

In Ephesians 5:31–32, the phrase "one flesh" is said to be a mystery that relates to Christ and the church. The relationship between Christ and the church doesn't involve sexual union or anatomical difference. While the church is described as the bride of Christ in Revelation 19 and 21, the church is made up of both men and women. The nuptial language is symbolic. The Bible employs marital imagery, not to sexualize our relationship with Christ, but to emphasize how God brings us into his loving embrace. Not only does Ephesians 5 never mention gender-based anatomical differences, it focuses instead on the fact that husbands and wives are part of the *same* body. "The husband is the head of the wife as Christ is the head of the church, his body.... In this same way, husbands ought to love their wives as their own bodies" (Ephesians 5:23, 28).[11]

So based on Ephesians, gender difference isn't necessary to become one flesh in the Bible's understanding of those words. What *is* necessary is that two lives are joined as one in the context of a binding covenant.

THE DIFFERENCE THAT MATTERS

It makes sense that, if marriage is a reflection of Christ and the church, it should require *some* kind of difference between the partners. Christ and the church are not the same, after all. But neither are any two people the same. The Bible gives us no reason to think *gender* difference is the specific difference that's necessary to illustrate Christ's covenantal love for the church.

You may have heard the argument that same-sex love is a function of narcissism, because it involves seeking romantic fulfillment in one who is like oneself. But this is a narrow understanding of difference, and it's not supported by Scripture. What seems to me to be most important in marriage is not whether the partners are anatomically different from one another. It's whether the inherently different people involved are willing to keep covenant with each other in a relationship of mutual self-giving.

Differences in personality, passions, careers, goals, and needs are the differences that require each partner's self-sacrifice, which reflects Christ's sacrificial love for us. Those kinds of differences, when valued and sacrificed for, bring the Bible's basis for marriage to life. Same-sex couples can and do live out that deepest sense of difference.

Granted, every kind of sexual love, including same-sex love, *can* be narcissistic if the partners approach it in selfish ways. But I think it's the flawed understanding of sex as a "reunion" of two incomplete halves that's most likely to foster a selfish attitude. If marriage is viewed primarily as a path to completing oneself, then it risks becoming self-absorbed. Marriage is designed to be a human reflection of the only love that offers true completion: God's love for us in Christ.[12]

In God's glorious, limitless love, he has imparted to us that most precious and humbling of gifts: our own capacity for love. Not all Christians are called to marriage, and the church should uphold the validity of celibacy for those who are called to it. But for those who do *not* sense a calling to celibacy, God's gift of sexual love in marriage should be affirmed. There is no biblical reason to exclude the covenantal bonds of gay Christians from that affirmation.

My parents' marriage of more than thirty years has set an example for me. My mom and dad have come to see that same-sex marriage doesn't undermine the institution that has been so meaningful to them. And in fact, it's now one of their deepest prayers to see me share in the joy and commitment of marriage with the support of a thriving Christian community.

If that day comes, I will treasure their wholehearted celebration.

What the Image of God Teaches Us About Gay Christians

I f you walk around the heart of Harvard's campus, you'll come across a building emblazoned with this inscription: "What is man that thou art mindful of him?"

The quote comes from Psalm 8, a meditation on the wonders of God's creation and the fact that God cares for us despite our smallness in light of the immensity of the universe. For a secular school like Harvard, the prominence of that religious language is noteworthy. But even more noteworthy is the building the inscription adorns: the philosophy department, where any claims to objective truth are met with fierce scrutiny.

And yet, even in such a highly intellectual setting, one truth about the human condition still seems to find widespread acceptance: While we are infinitesimally small in the grand scheme of things, we also have intrinsic value. This belief is shared in some form by many cultures and worldviews, and as the above quote from the Psalms illustrates, it is deeply embedded in the Christian faith. The Bible teaches that, as human beings, we are made in the image of God, and that fact forms the basis of our inherent value.

In previous chapters, we looked at a biblical case for affirming gay Christians as equals—in sexuality, community, and marriage. In making that case, we considered the big-picture issues of experience, tradition, celibacy, marriage, and the six Scripture passages that refer to same-sex behavior.

In this chapter, I want to look at the issue of sexuality in a very different way. I want to address the same questions and approach the same conversation with an eye toward what makes us human and what it means—on a deeper level—that we *are* human.

For the purposes of our discussion, I'd like to consider the biblical doctrine of the image of God more carefully. In what ways are we made in God's image, and what does that mean for all of us, and for gay Christians in particular? If same-sex orientation is consistent with the image of God, how would that affect our bigger discussion of long-term, committed same-sex relationships?

THE MEANING OF BEING MADE IN GOD'S IMAGE

In Genesis 1, we read that, after the creation of the heavens, the earth, plants, and animals, God created humanity.

> Then God said, "Let us make mankind in our image, in our likeness, so that they may rule over the fish in the sea and the birds in the sky, over the livestock and all the wild animals, and over all the creatures that move along the ground."
>
> So God created mankind in his own image, in the image of God he created them; male and female he created them.
> (Genesis 1:26–27)

Did you notice the repetition? In those two sentences, Scripture states the big idea three times: humans are created in the image of God. All of God's creation is "very good" (Genesis 1:31), but only humans are said to be made in God's image. It is that likeness to God, according to Scripture, that gives humans our intrinsic value.

In Genesis 9:6, we see God prohibiting murder based on the fact that we are made in his image. Our likeness to God is also why James forbade cursing others. He wrote, "With the tongue we praise our Lord and Father, and with it we curse human beings, who have been made in God's likeness" (James 3:9).

To kill or to curse a human being is an offense against the Creator as well as against a creature. And while that holds true for all abuses of creation, including animal mistreatment and environmental degradation, the Bible tells us that it carries singular weight in the case of offenses against humans.

But what is it, exactly, that constitutes the image of God in each of us?

DOES THE IMAGE REQUIRE HETEROSEXUALITY?

On this question, the Christian tradition has offered a range of responses. Augustine and Thomas Aquinas (fourth and thirteenth centuries) argued that the image of God was found in a person's intellect or reason. Ambrose and Calvin (fourth and sixteenth centuries) said, instead, that it consisted in the human soul. Irenaeus (second century) agreed that human reason was part of the image of God, but he believed free will was part of it too.[1]

More recently, some theologians have advanced an understanding of the image of God that has particular relevance to our conversation in this book. Karl Barth argued in the mid-twentieth century that God's image is most fully found in *the union of male and female*. Barth wrote, "As a man [one] can only be genuinely human with woman, or as a woman with man."[2] That argument continues to influence the thinking of many non-affirming Christians, who frequently suggest that the fullness of God's image is uniquely found in heterosexual marriage.[3]

But is that understanding of God's image correct? It's true that Genesis 1:27 describes our creation as "male and female." And in Genesis 1:28, God said to "be fruitful and increase in number," an act which requires the union of male and female.

Yet two aspects of Genesis 1 point to a different understanding of the image of God, an understanding that is not unique to heterosexuality. First, God's image is found only in humans, but gender difference also exists among animals. In Genesis 1:22, God gave a procreative blessing to animals that is similar to the one he gave to humanity: "Be fruitful and increase in number and fill the water in the seas, and let the birds increase on the earth." Given that our identity as God's image bearers is what sets us *apart* from the rest of creation, it doesn't make sense to say that God's image is uniquely found in something we have in common with so many other creatures.

What's more, Genesis 1 focuses on something else—and something that *is* unique to humans—when describing the image of God: our dominion over creation. Genesis 1:26 explicitly links God's image to human dominion: "Let us make mankind in our image, in our likeness, *so that* they may rule over the fish in the sea and the birds in the sky, over the livestock and all the wild animals, and over all the creatures that move along the ground." This theme is repeated in verse 28, after the creation of humanity: "Be fruitful and increase in number; fill the earth and subdue it. Rule over the fish in the sea and the birds in the sky and over every living creature that moves on the ground."

Based on the text of Genesis 1, it seems that the image of God has a greater connection to our dominion over creation than to heterosexual relationships. And as New Testament scholar James Brownson has written, the reference to "male and female" in Genesis 1:27—"in the image of God he created them; male and female he created them"— most likely means "that both male and female are created in the divine image…[and] that all the dignity, honor, and significance of bearing the divine image belong equally to men and to women."[4]

Like Genesis 1, the psalm we looked at above also connects our likeness to God with our dominion over creation—not to the sexual union of men and women. In Psalm 8:5–8, we read: "Yet you have made them a little lower than God, and crowned them with glory and honor. You have given them dominion over the works of your hands; you have put all things under their feet, all sheep and oxen, and also the beasts of the field, the birds of the air, and the fish of the sea, whatever passes along the paths of the seas" (NRSV).[5]

In the New Testament, we find an even more foundational reason why the image of God can't uniquely be tied to heterosexuality. According to 2 Corinthians 4:4 and Colossians 1:15, Jesus himself *is* the image of God. If heterosexual union were required to complete the image of God, how could Jesus be the "exact representation" of God's being (see Hebrews 1:3)?

This isn't to say that nothing about opposite-sex relationships can bear God's image. In many ways, they can and often do show us something of God's nature. But saying that the only intimate relationships that can reflect God's image are those between a man and a woman misses the Bible's bigger picture of what his image encompasses.

The New Testament calls us to be like God by living a righteous and holy life (see Ephesians 4:24). It also tells us to reflect God's nature to the world by showing forgiveness and love (see Matthew 6:14–15; John 13:34–35). Ephesians 5:1–2 specifically links our call to "be imitators of God" with the command to "live a life of love, just as Christ loved us" (NIV 1984).

We can share all those traits to some extent with God. So aren't they, too, part of what it means for us to be his image bearers? As 1 John 4:19 reminds us, "We love because he first loved us." And the same is true of our capacity for forgiveness, compassion, and self-sacrifice.

As Dick Staub noted in his book *About You,* when we return to the full creation narrative of Genesis 1, we can identify a variety of ways that we reflect God's nature. Just as God creates, we, too, are creative. As God is Spirit, we have spiritual aspects as well. And as God thinks and speaks, we also have unique gifts of intelligence and abilities to communicate. God's image can't be reduced to just one trait. Many characteristics, from love to creativity to forgiveness, contribute to forming his image in us.[6]

OUR IMPRINTED NEED FOR RELATIONSHIP

One characteristic that we share to some extent with God is particularly important for thinking about sexual orientation, and it's also highlighted in Genesis 1: The triune God exists in relationship. As humans, we are also relational beings.

In Genesis 1:26, God did not say, "Let me make mankind in my image, in my likeness." He said instead, "Let *us* make mankind in *our* image, in *our* likeness." God's nature is relational because God is Trini-

tarian: Father, Son, and Holy Spirit. In the words of theologian Anthony Hoekema, God is a "being in fellowship."[7]

God's creation of each one of us reflects his triune, relational nature. So it shouldn't surprise us that the need for relationship is deeply
imprinted in human beings. We see that need recognized as early as
Genesis 2:18, when God declares that "it is not good for the man to be
alone." And while human relationship can take many forms—community, friends, family, romantic love—it's difficult to imagine life
without it. As Karl Barth wrote, "God is in relationship, and so too is
the man created by Him. This is his divine likeness."[8]

It's telling that, in his novel *The Great Divorce,* C. S. Lewis used
extreme isolation to characterize one aspect of hell. He described how,
in the process of choosing to live thousands of miles away from everyone else, people began to lose their humanity.[9]

Lewis was right: a life devoid of relational connection couldn't be a
fully human one. Now, it's true that deep, fulfilling relationships don't
have to be sexual. Certainly, sexual union isn't necessary to live a fully
human life. After all, Jesus lived the fullest life of anyone, and he was
celibate.

But as humans, our sexuality is a core part of who we are. It's part
of what it means to be a relational person. Whether we ever pursue romantic relationships, our awareness of ourselves as sexual beings and
our longing for intimacy profoundly influence how we relate to others.

Of course, the desire for sex isn't unique to humans. But our sexual
drive does point us to what *is* unique about human sexuality: our potential to discipline and sanctify our sexual desires through a covenantal
bond. What we could experience as more of an animalistic drive for
self-gratification can instead be transformed into a powerful bonding

agent in the context of marriage. Through the covenantal potential of our sexuality, we can reflect the image of our relational, covenant-keeping God.

CREATED TO BE IN COVENANT

In that sense, it's true that opposite-sex unions can reflect God's image. At their best, they help show his covenantal love for us. But why can same-sex unions not do the same?

Non-affirming Christians often think of same-sex orientation as a mere code word for disordered or sinful sexual desires, but that perspective overlooks a critical aspect of what it means to be gay. Sexual orientation involves much more than just sexual attraction. For both gay and straight people, it also encompasses our capacity to channel our physical attractions into a lifelong covenant with another person.

That covenant-keeping capacity is essential to who we are as creatures made in God's image. As Barth has argued, God created us so that we could be in covenant with him.[10] Because same-sex orientation contains the potential for self-giving, covenantal love, it's consistent with the image of God in us.

In light of that understanding, the question we should ask is not whether it is acceptable for the church to deny gay Christians the possibility of sexual fulfillment in marriage. Instead, we should ask: *Is it acceptable to deny gay Christians the opportunity to* sanctify *their sexual desires through a God-reflecting covenant?*[11]

This, of course, is no idle question. In practice, condemning gay Christians' potential for covenantal love has been deeply destructive. For many, it's corroded the core sense of worth they should have as people created in God's image.

Let me share the story of Rob and Linda Robertson, a Christian couple from Seattle I've come to know. Their story is heart wrenching, but their actions and attitudes as parents demonstrated deep, unconditional love.

When he was twelve, their son Ryan told them he was attracted to boys, not girls. They let Ryan know that they deeply loved him. "We will *always* love you. And this is hard. *Really* hard. But we know what God says about this, so you are going to have to make some really difficult choices.... You are going to have to choose to follow Jesus, no matter what. And since you know what the Bible says, and since you want to follow God, embracing your sexuality is *not* an option."[12]

For the next six years, Linda and Rob repeated that message. They also went out of their way to try to help their son. They gave him books about overcoming sexual temptation, encouraged him to build deep friendships with straight guys, and helped him find spiritual nourishment and support at the church youth group. Ryan, for his part, worked every day to overcome his desires, wanting desperately to please God and his parents. But as years passed and nothing changed, Ryan began to feel overwhelmed by anguish and hopelessness.

So around age eighteen, feeling depressed, suicidal, and rejected by God, he turned to drugs in a desperate search for any kind of relief. He told his parents, "Mom, I want you and Dad to know that I have been researching hallucinogens, and I am going to try using them to see if I can find some peace." He left home, and for the next year and a half, his family didn't know where he was. By the time he contacted them, their earlier fear about his sexual orientation had been replaced with the desire simply to see him again and let him know he was loved—"No buts. No conditions. Just because he breathes." Fortunately, Ryan did come back, and over the next ten months, they were able to repair much that had been damaged in their relationship. But after ten months in recovery, Ryan relapsed—and overdosed—while spending an evening with old friends. He spent the next seventeen days in intensive care, and died on July 16, 2009, at age twenty.

Rob and Linda's world was shattered. As Linda wrote, "We had unintentionally taught Ryan to hate his sexuality. And since sexuality cannot be separated from the self, we had taught Ryan to hate himself.... What we had wished for, prayed for, hoped for—that we would *not* have a gay son—came true. But not at all in the way we had envisioned."[13]

Rob and Linda loved their son dearly, and they worked hard to show that to him. But even when they expressed their beliefs as compassionately as they did, their non-affirming understanding of homosexuality ultimately led Ryan to a place of despair and tragic self-harm.

Yes, plenty of Christian teachings are hard for us to live out. But no other teaching that Christians widely continue to embrace has caused anything like the torment, destruction, and alienation from God that the church's rejection of same-sex relationships has caused. If we tell people that their *every* desire for intimate, sexual bonding is shameful and disordered, we encourage them to hate a core part of who they were created to be. And if we reject the desires of gay Christians to express their sexuality within a lifelong covenant, we separate them from our covenantal God, and we tarnish their ability to bear his image.

SEXUAL ORIENTATION, SIN, AND THE GOOD NEWS

I want to be clear: Affirming that same-sex orientation is consistent with the image of God does not mean watering down the doctrine of sin. Sin is what separates each of us from God. Sin also mars the image of God in our being. But strikingly, those aren't the consequences of affirming lifelong, monogamous same-sex unions. They are the consequences of *rejecting* all same-sex relationships.

It's true, some churches have shied away from emphasizing the doctrine of sin, in part because of how they've seen it harm the lesbian, gay, bisexual, and transgender people in their midst. For some Christians—and for many people outside the church—the language of sin can sound judgmental, intolerant, and out of touch.

But just because a doctrine has been *misused* doesn't mean it's no longer true. From our earliest years of life, we know something is wrong in the world. And even though we might prefer to lay the blame at the feet of others, we know that we often contribute to the problem ourselves. We harbor an innate tendency to advance our self-interest at the expense of others. As God told Cain in Genesis 4:7, "If you do not do what is right, sin is crouching at your door; it desires to have you, but you must rule over it."

We can never master sin on our own. Our impulses toward anger, greed, or self-glorification can be overwhelming. Time and again, we fall prey to temptation. Jesus said that "everyone who sins is a slave to sin" (John 8:34), and our experiences agonizingly show that to be true. As the Bible puts it, "There is no one righteous, not even one" (Romans 3:10).

But while we are far from perfect, God *is* perfect, and he created humans to live in perfect peace and harmony. Yet we prefer our own ways over God's ways all too often. Given how much destruction we cause, we deserve to endure the consequences. But God lavished his grace on us. He took on human flesh in the person of Christ, and after living a sinless life, Jesus chose to take the sins of the world upon him-self. As Romans 3:25 explains, "God presented Christ as a sacrifice of atonement, through the shedding of his blood—to be received by faith." Through his atoning death on the cross, Jesus made possible what our sinful choices had prevented: our ability to live in right rela-tionship with God.

By placing our faith in God's saving grace that Jesus made available to us, we can live in harmony with God—not because we deserve to, but because God has offered us reconciliation. As Jesus and the earliest Christians preached, a core part of how we respond to that gift should involve turning away from our destructive habits, or repenting from our sins. If we're truly grateful for Christ's sacrifice, which washed away our sins, then we can't continue to embrace sin. Paul wrote that "our old self was crucified with [Christ] so that the body ruled by sin might be done away with, that we should no longer be slaves to sin" (Romans 6:6).[14]

As the Holy Spirit works within us to help us live in ways pleasing to God, we can begin to reflect God's image more fully. We can more fully demonstrate God's character in the world, helping to fulfill our created purpose of bringing God glory on earth. Our lives, then, be-come a witness to the transforming power of the gospel—its power to reconcile, redeem, and renew.

AFFIRMING GOD'S GOOD CREATION

Admittedly, we reflect God imperfectly. But we remain God's unique image bearers. With the help of the Holy Spirit, Christians have taken off their "old self with its practices and have put on the new self, which is being renewed in knowledge in the image of its Creator" (Colossians

3:9–10). As Ephesians 4:24 explains, our new self was "created to be like God in true righteousness and holiness."

We won't experience perfect righteousness and holiness until the resurrection of our bodies. But even though we won't fully embody God's image until then,[15] the Holy Spirit empowers us now to "reflect the Lord's glory" and to be "transformed into his likeness with ever-increasing glory" (2 Corinthians 3:18, NIV 1984). Even now, there is something of God's image in every person. All people, Christians and non-Christians, gay and straight, are made in the image of God, and we are all designed to reflect his nature.

In light of that reality, lesbian, gay, bisexual, and transgender people have inestimable dignity and worth. So how could the suffering they endure when their families and churches don't affirm them express God's intentions toward his creation? Affirming same-sex relationships wouldn't change the Bible's core truths about sin, repentance, and redemption. In fact, given that same-sex orientation is consistent with God's image, affirming same-sex relationships is the only way to *defend* those truths with clarity, coherence, and persuasiveness.

As we seek to discern right from wrong, we have no better guide than God's character as revealed in Scripture. Based on our discussion in this chapter, same-sex orientation is in keeping with God's relational, covenant-keeping character. That means we should understand it as a created characteristic—not as a distortion caused by the fall. By branding same-sex orientation broken, we are wrongly rejecting a good part of God's creation. And with awful consequences, we are tarnishing the image of God in Ryan Robertson and so many others like him.

Instead of making gay Christians more like God, as turning from genuine sin would do, embracing a non-affirming position makes them less like God. So it isn't gay Christians who are sinning against God by entering into monogamous, loving relationships. It is the church that is sinning against them by rejecting their intimate relationships.

But if the church were to bless committed same-sex unions for gay Christians, we would advance God's sanctifying purposes for their lives. Until then, we are distorting the image of God, not only in the lives of gay Christians, but in the church as a whole.

Seeds of a Modern Reformation

I n July 2010, seven months after I came out to my dad, he told me he was making some changes. One of the most surprising was his decision not to renew his membership in a national organization for Christian lawyers.

"Why's that?" I asked.

"I no longer agree with their position on gay Christians," Dad said.

Fighting back tears, I gave him a giant hug. Over the course of seven months, Dad's willingness to study this issue had led him to profoundly change his views. Now, he was putting himself on the line for gay Christians—and for me. He hadn't changed his belief in the authority of the Bible, but he had changed his understanding of the key Bible passages and their historical context. For Dad, that meant taking action.

Over the next year, my dad became an increasingly vocal advocate for gay Christians, beginning at our church, where he was an elder. His new viewpoint didn't sway the elder board, and it caused tension for him with a number of his friends. Yet his forthrightness and gentle spirit opened the door to some important conversations. My mom and I, too, had our share of heartfelt discussions with friends.

Members of our church community began to engage on a personal level with an issue many of them hadn't seriously considered before. Some were open to conversation but felt unable to change at the time. And some, after taking a closer look at Scripture, embarked on a process of moderating or changing their long-held views. A few of our friends, we found out, were already quietly supportive of gay Christians, but they didn't feel it was something they could speak openly about in church. We'd never have known their views without starting the conversation.

Even for those who didn't change their position, a seed was planted. For the first time, many of them became aware of a theologically conservative, biblically rigorous understanding that differed radically from what they had always assumed was the "Christian" position. For the first time, many of our friends saw faithful Christian parents affirm their gay son in both his faith and his desire for a committed same-sex relationship.

At about that time, our church's denomination voted to approve the ordination of non-celibate gay clergy. Unfortunately, that move sparked enough backlash that our congregation decided to leave our denomination and join one that is strongly non-affirming. Despite the positive dialogue we'd started with many of our close friends, our church as a whole wasn't willing to engage in that conversation. After it became painfully clear that our church wouldn't be a supportive community for me anytime in the near future, my family and I reluctantly left.

Tragically, I hear from many lesbian, gay, bisexual, and transgender Christians whose churches also are convinced that they cannot take an affirming approach to same-sex relationships while remaining faithful to Scripture.

I wrote this book to show that there is a third way. The message of Scripture for gay Christians is not what non-affirming Christians assume it to be.

What can affirming Christians do to be agents of transformation on this central issue of our time? You can walk in the light you now have. You can speak the truth, beginning with your most powerful instrument of change—your life.

Since coming out, I've met Christians from all walks of life who have made significant personal sacrifices to show God's love to LGBT people. Their stories are an inspiration and an example to others who want to integrate their love for God with their compassion for marginalized and mistreated people.

I'd like to introduce you to three remarkable Christians whose lives hold lessons for us all.

THE STORY OF KATHY BALDOCK

Kathy Baldock homeschooled her two children in Reno, Nevada, and she was actively involved in her church. Like other Christians she knew, she didn't think it was possible for a person to be both Christian and gay. "The issue didn't affect my life," she said, "and I thought I knew what the Bible said about it, so I had no reason to question my views."

Then, while out hiking, she met Netto. Kathy suspected Netto might be gay, but that didn't prevent her from striking up a friendship. In time, Netto came out to Kathy. As a Native American and a woman, Netto already felt counted out by much of society. But as a lesbian, she told Kathy, even God didn't love her.

Their friendship helped soften Kathy's heart toward gay people, but she still believed that homosexuality was a sin. Several years later, she read an article about the Gay Christian Network. She was intrigued by the idea of an organization for gay Christians—could anyone really be gay *and* Christian? she wondered—so she decided to attend their annual conference to find out. There, she watched silently as four hundred gay Christians worshiped God. The experience transformed her, and back in Reno, she kept meeting more gay believers, many of whom had been disowned by their families and shown the door by their churches.

Kathy was convinced these encounters were the work of the Holy Spirit, and she felt called to reexamine her opposition to gay relationships. "I didn't revise any Bible passages," she said. "I revisited the Bible and came to a more accurate understanding of it." After a year of prayer and study, she came to the same conclusion that my dad would reach several years later: the biblical injunctions against same-sex behavior don't envision or encompass the committed relationships of gay Christians.

Kathy was brokenhearted over the pain and suffering the church had caused. She decided to follow God's call to help reform the church. She attended gay pride parades across the country, where she offered a Christian voice of love and affirmation to counter the condemnation of many street preachers. Kathy would wear a T-shirt that read "Hurt by Church? Get a Straight Apology Here."

She has since become a tireless advocate for gay Christians in conservative churches. Her children are straight, but through her ministry, she has become a spiritual mother to hundreds of lesbian, gay, bisexual, and transgender people. She's helped restore dozens of broken relationships between parents and children. Most importantly, Kathy has nurtured countless LGBT people back to faith in Christ.

In recent years, she's developed a particular heart for transgender

Christians. While sexual orientation is becoming increasingly well understood, the issue of gender identity remains confusing for many. For transgender people, as Kathy came to understand it, "The brain stamp does not match the sex assigned at birth. The brain says the person is one gender, and the body presents as the other sex."

As a trans Christian friend of mine, Mateo, explained his experience, "I've always felt male, but it seemed like my body was betraying me. Coming out as trans released me from years of crippling shame and depression. I've never felt closer to God or more deeply loved by my creator."

It's easy for some Christians to reject transgender identity as somehow at odds with God's creation of humanity as male and female. But as Kathy has learned, glib responses do not do justice to the lives, faith, and experiences of transgender people. Few groups are more misunderstood, mistreated, or unwelcome in the church today. Trans people are not rebelling. Like people who are gay or bisexual, they are simply created differently.[1]

Kathy Baldock never imagined she would become a passionate advocate for LGBT Christians. But by submitting to God's call, she has become a light in the darkness for many who have felt rejected by Jesus. Through her nonprofit organization, Canyonwalker Connections, and her book, *Walking the Bridgeless Canyon,* Kathy's servant leadership continues to bring healing and hope to many who need them most.

THE STORY OF DR. JAMES BROWNSON

Dr. James Brownson is a professor of New Testament at Western Theological Seminary in Holland, Michigan. Brownson has taught future clergy and lay leaders in the Reformed Church in America (RCA) for more than twenty-five years. He is so widely respected as a biblical scholar that the RCA gave him its highest title for trusted thinkers and teachers.

In 2005, Brownson published a journal article expressing sympathy for gay Christians. But he stopped there, making clear that he was an evangelical Christian who was fully committed to Scripture. He added, "God's intention for human sexuality is that it find full expression only in the covenant of marriage between a man and a woman. I do not believe 'gay marriage' to be sanctioned by Scripture."

The following year, though, the issue became much more personal for him: his son, then a senior in high school, came out. As Brownson would later write:

> I wish I could say that, since I had always been such a thoughtful and empathic scholar, when I was faced with this case in my own family, I would simply find the conclusions I had already arrived at…to be adequate. But I must confess—to my regret and embarrassment—that this was not the case. I realized, in fact, that my former work had stayed at a level of abstraction that wasn't helpful when it came to the concrete and specific questions I faced with my son.[2]

As a biblical theologian, Brownson felt called to return to Scripture in order to discern God's will for his son. He realized that his earlier conclusions were removed from the lives of gay Christians, making them impracticable. For instance, while he'd formerly made a clear distinction between "same-sex orientation" and "same-sex behavior," he began to understand that being gay cannot be compartmentalized so easily. Like heterosexuality, gay people's sexuality is a core part of what it means for them to be human. Attempts to extinguish it often result in destructive, emotionally crippling ways of living.

After years of prayer, reflection, and meticulous examination of the Scriptures, Brownson realized his previous conclusions were not truly faithful to God's Word. At that point, his main concern was not with his reputation or his career, but with the integrity of the body of Christ. He decided to invite other Christians into a conversation about Scripture and same-sex relationships.

In 2013, Brownson took that conversation national. He published a book, *Bible, Gender, Sexuality: Reframing the Church's Debate on Same-Sex Relationships,* which is easily one of the finest theological treatments of this issue. Brownson's biblical analysis is extraordinarily careful and thorough, and his uncompromising fidelity to the authority of Scripture is a gift for all Christians who want to take the Bible's teachings seriously.

Rather than focusing primarily on the six passages related to same-sex behavior, Brownson offers a comprehensive survey of the foundations of gender and sexuality in Scripture. In particular, he overturns the core claims of Robert Gagnon, the most influential non-affirming scholar. By challenging Gagnon's argument about gender complementarity, Brownson is changing the conversation among church leaders and biblical scholars.

But Brownson has done much more than refute arguments. He's also laid the foundations for a positive, "cross-cultural" vision for Christian sexual ethics. That vision centers on the biblical language of a "one-flesh" marriage union, emphasizing the ways marriage should honor spouses while also enriching and supporting their churches and communities. By presenting a deeply biblical foundation for sexual ethics, Brownson is contributing to an even larger undertaking. He is helping to ensure that, as the church comes to affirm same-sex relationships, we develop an even richer love for God and his Word.

Brownson's work is a blessing to Christians. Equally important, his humility, grace, and compassion are examples for all believers.

THE STORY OF JUSTIN LEE

Gay Christians need positive role models as much as straight Christians do, and few have taken on that role as effectively as Justin Lee. Born and raised in Raleigh, North Carolina, Justin has been passionate about his faith from a young age. As a teenager, though, he realized he was attracted to other boys. He was convinced his feelings were wrong, so he worked diligently to change them.

After high school, Justin shared his struggle with his parents, who were concerned but loving. He spent the next few years working with "ex-gay" organizations that tried to change his sexual orientation. But those experiences were both damaging and counterproductive, as he detailed in his book *Torn: Rescuing the Gospel from the Gays-vs.-Christians Debate.*

Justin had always enjoyed a strong relationship with his dad, but some "ex-gay" groups refused to believe it. Instead, they tried to convince him that his father had been a failure, which helped explain why Justin had developed same-sex attractions. As he wrote in his book, "What kind of ministry takes a person who thinks he has a wonderful relationship with his father and convinces him that he actually has a bad one? This was feeling less and less like the work of God to me."[3]

Over time, Justin realized that the "ex-gay" movement was pointing to questionable breakthroughs—and tissue-thin examples—as success stories. The people being held up as role models still experienced significant same-sex attraction, and many struggled to manufacture even a hint of heterosexual desire. But those who left behind same-sex promiscuity for a heterosexual marriage were heralded as having "overcome" being gay, despite the fact that they continued to experience same-sex attractions. For Justin, who was committed to abstinence until marriage, those stories only confirmed his growing anxiety that the church had no real answers for him.

Undeterred, he sought involvement in Christian fellowships during his time at college. His faith in ex-gay ministries had been shaken, but his faith in God had not. But Christian fellowships at his college treated him coldly. He wasn't in a relationship, but the fact that he was gay unnerved ministry leaders. When he encouraged them to show greater sensitivity to gay people, they told him to leave his "agenda" at home.

After years of dismissive treatment, it would be understandable if Justin's story ended with disillusionment, or even a loss of faith. But instead, he started a ministry for gay Christians, many of whom were facing similar isolation and hardship. His ministry began modestly, as an online message board for Christians struggling with their sexual orientation. Some were in same-sex relationships. Others felt called to celibacy.

Eventually, Justin's message board, called the Gay Christian Network, connected enough people that they decided to meet. Since 2005, the Gay Christian Network has held an annual conference. By providing a safe space for LGBT Christians, the conferences offer much-needed community support for those who haven't found it in church. It was this conference that would open Kathy Baldock's eyes to the lives of gay Christians, sparking years of passionate advocacy on their behalf.

Like Kathy and Dr. James Brownson, Justin has changed his views about the Bible and homosexuality, and he now affirms same-sex relationships. Also like them, he has not changed his fundamental commitment to the authority of Scripture. He's earned a reputation for being unfailingly gracious, patient, and respectful to everyone he encounters, no matter the person's viewpoint. His grace-filled approach to dialogue has made him uniquely effective at his work.

Justin is not the only person whose advocacy efforts have eroded the credibility of the ex-gay movement. But his work has been particularly influential in shifting the tide on that damaging practice, and his book *Torn* deserves a careful reading by anyone who doubts the permanence of same-sex orientation. Justin's life is a testament to the fact that gay Christians can have a vibrant faith, a rigorous personal ethic, and a Christlike approach to dialogue and disagreement.

THE REFORMATION PROJECT

Kathy, James, and Justin are far from alone. Countless others are also living out their faith by working for the acceptance and inclusion of LGBT people.

When I was trying to engage my church in a dialogue on this subject, I ended up feeling alone. I was grateful to have the support of my parents, without which I can't imagine having been able to make a larger effort. But most of our friends who were privately supportive didn't feel comfortable taking a public stand on the issue.

After posting a video online of a speech I gave on this subject, I heard similar stories from other Christians around the world. That's why, in 2013, I launched an organization called The Reformation Project. The organization's mission is to identify and empower Christians who are committed to making their churches affirming places for LGBT people. In the fall of 2013, a group of committed Christians gathered for our inaugural leadership training conference.

For a number of people in the group, the conference was the first time they'd met other Christians who were doing similar work. Many of them had only recently come to their theological position, so they were still in close contact with non-affirming Christians. That gave them a unique opportunity to open up the dialogue, but it also carried a burden of isolation. Simply coming together with other reformers, as we called them, was an empowering experience.

As the group knew, though, challenging days lay ahead. They'd committed to serve as visible and accessible voices for reform in their church communities. In churches like the one I grew up in, that work can be thankless and emotionally taxing.

One straight woman at the conference told me she wished her husband and others at her church could see what she was seeing: LGBT and straight Christians worshiping God together and diving into his Word with passion, reverence, and awe. (Fortunately, they now can see it. Much of the conference was recorded. Lectures and interviews can be viewed online at www.reformationproject.org.)

That group from the conference is already making a difference, and The Reformation Project is just getting started. Our goal is to ensure that all Christians, LGBT and straight, have the support they need to stay in their churches and receive affirmation when they or their loved ones come out. And while organizational support is critical, *any* Christian can take practical action steps in places where LGBT people are not affirmed. I invite you to pray about integrating these steps into your life in the months ahead.

Share Your Views Publicly

It's difficult to overstate the impact of this first step. Share your supportive views with others—with your Bible study group, over dinner with friends, on social media. A public affirmation of your support for LGBT people can make a huge difference.

Chances are good that your church, no matter how small, has some members who are lesbian, gay, bisexual, or transgender. Even if the issue has never been raised, you almost certainly have friends and family who are feeling isolated and alone *because* it has never been raised. Hiding one's sexual orientation from others is psychologically crippling, and it can cause depression and shame, even leading to serious thoughts of suicide. For many LGBT people, the first time they heard someone in their family or church say they would accept a person regardless of sexual orientation was what helped bring them back from a place of crushing self-hatred.

If you are not yet ready to affirm same-sex relationships, publicly stating that you are open to reconsidering the issue can still make a world of difference. If you make that kind of a statement, you will likely hear from friends and loved ones expressing relief and gratitude that they finally have someone they can talk to. You can play a significant role in changing the damaging status quo of silence.

Talk with Your Pastor and Church Leaders

Many pastors fear that any discussion of LGBT Christians will cause division and tension within their congregation. Ask to meet with your pastor and other church leaders one-on-one to start the conversation. Let them know why you think it's important that they explicitly mention LGBT believers from the pulpit, and offer to help them start a dialogue about it. Even if church leaders are uncomfortable with same-sex relationships, you can help them see that gay people can be Christians in every sense of the word and should feel safe, welcome, and valued in your church.

Lead a Bible Study About Gay Christians

Others in your church will have questions and concerns about the Bible's stance on same-sex relationships. Engage those concerns with sensitivity and respect. Some friends, family members, and pastors will likely think that affirming same-sex relationships would require them to give up their commitment to the authority of Scripture. That's why I encourage you to lead a careful study of Scripture before asking people to change their position.

Invite church members to participate in a Bible study to explore the issue. Use this book as a guide, or make use of James Brownson's book *Bible, Gender, Sexuality.* As you study and discuss, bring the focus back to the people affected by the church's stance. If some people are convinced same-sex relationships are sinful, ask them to consider what that viewpoint means for gay Christians. Do they feel that mandatory celibacy bears good fruit in the lives of gay Christians? How closely have they walked alongside gay brothers and sisters who have tried to take that path, and have they seen the consequences it produced? Even if disagreement persists, you can help foster greater openness, compassion, and understanding toward LGBT people.

Start a Support Group for LGBT Christians

Even when a church is non-affirming, some LGBT believers are worshiping there. They need as much understanding and support as you can offer. Start a support group for church members who are gay, bisexual, or transgender or who are questioning their sexual orientation or gender identity. Help create a safe space for them to share their experiences, frustrations, and doubts. While some church members might be uncomfortable with openly acknowledging the presence of LGBT people, it's vital that the support groups are announced and people welcomed. That sends the message to young people in particular that, even if the church is wrestling with the issue, they will not be cast out if they tell others about their feelings.

If You Are Lesbian, Gay, Bisexual, or Transgender, Come Out

Coming out is one of the hardest things you will ever do, but it's also one of the most rewarding and freeing. If you are concerned about threats to your physical safety or whether you'll be kicked out of your home, waiting to come out until you feel more safe—even if that may be years away—is likely the wisest approach. But while you should approach the timing of your coming out carefully, Christians have a duty to be honest. Choosing to be open about your sexual orientation or gender identity is important not only for you. Your courage will make a difference for others who are afraid to come out, and it will open the door to a stronger, more peaceful relationship with Christ.

Coming out is also an act of grace and trust to the straight Christians in your life who love you. Don't write them off, even based on insensitive things they may have said in the past. Give them a chance to learn and grow, and you may be surprised at their openness. Watching someone's heart and mind change—especially out of love for you—is a profound blessing.

Take Some Risks

Coming out as an LGBT Christian or as an LGBT-affirming Christian can carry significant risks. It could jeopardize your career and your reputation, and could cost you a number of friends. Again, be prudent, and do your best to put together a robust support system in advance.

But ultimately, there are things that matter more than our reputations, and our faithfulness to Christ is undoubtedly one of them.

Jesus didn't command us to care for the least of these only when it's convenient or when our reputation isn't on the line. He told us to lay down our lives for our friends (see John 15:13). That kind of sacrifice isn't easy or convenient. But God's image will be tarnished until LGBT believers are welcomed as a full, thriving part of the body of Christ. As you seek to follow in Jesus's footsteps, I hope you will ask yourself: *What am I willing to sacrifice for my LGBT friends?*

Living that way requires that you take risks. Ultimately, comfort and convenience aren't what's most important. But as you help to advance God's kingdom through your courage and sacrifice, you will find that the risks are worth it.

THE WITNESS OF FLESH AND BLOOD

More than twenty-five years ago, a historian and gay Christian named John Boswell penned an essay on the power of personal testimony to change hearts and minds. Boswell argued that, even though God used written words to communicate with his people in the Old Testament, his ultimate self-revelation came in the form of Jesus. Drawing on the rich meaning of the Greek word *logos* in John 1:1, Boswell wrote:

> Christ was God's unanswerable "argument." His people had hardened their hearts against his spoken reasons, the arguments propounded—in *words*—for centuries by the prophets and sages. So he sent an argument in the form of a human being, a life, a person. The argument became flesh and blood: so real that no one could refute or ignore it.[4]

Gay Christians, Boswell continued, can follow in Christ's foot-steps. While they should engage the scriptural concerns of their brothers and sisters, reasoned argument has its limits. Ultimately, the most powerful case gay Christians can offer is the witness of their own lives. "It is much harder for most people to remain hostile to and unmoved by a living brother than it is to rail against an abstraction," Boswell concluded. "Gay Christians are *logoi* in this sense, arguments incarnated in persons…[who make] their commitment, their lives, their beings an unanswerable, living statement of faithfulness and love."[5]

His insights hold true for straight Christians too. If you are straight and choose to step out in faith to support LGBT brothers and sisters, you'll serve as a model for other Christians. By continuing to live in obedience to Jesus, you'll demonstrate that affirming LGBT people is not at odds with being a faithful Christian. As more believers are coming to realize, affirming our gay brothers and sisters isn't simply one possible path Christians can take. It isn't just a valid option. This kind of love and affirmation—regardless of sexual orientation or gender identity—is, in fact, a requirement of Christian faithfulness.

Acknowledgments

This book would not have been possible without the unfailing support and affirmation I received from my mom and dad. The vibrancy of my faith is directly attributable to the humble, authentic faith they lived out as I was growing up. I am so blessed to have them as my parents. My sister, Christine, has also been an invaluable support to me, both as a friend and as a wordsmith with a keen grasp on the craft of writing.

There can be no better literary agent in the business than Chris Parris-Lamb, who passionately believed in this book even before I did. Chris has been a remarkably kind, talented, and effective guide and advocate for me from day one. I am also tremendously grateful to David Kopp, whose meticulous edits made this book vastly better, and whose kind and gentle spirit made working with him a delight.

Every person at Convergent, Crown, and the Gernert Company who has had a hand in bringing this book to life has done a tremendous job. In particular, I want to thank Ron Lee, whose line edits were immensely helpful; Rachel Rokicki, Carisa Hayes, and Allison O'Hara for all their help with marketing and publicity; as well as Steve Cobb, Ken Petersen, and Carie Freimuth for their support.

I greatly appreciate the feedback of Jim Brownson, Dale Martin, and Martti Nissinen on my manuscript. Their work and their input significantly improved this book. I am also grateful for the help of my industrious research assistants, Hugo Marquez and Ian Leonard, as well as the assistance of Megan Rhinehart with the endnotes.

I am grateful every day for the sacrifices so many have made to help create a world in which I can even imagine a future for myself that includes a marriage and a family. I am blessed, too, by the support I have received from my extended family in this undertaking. And while I cannot list all the friends who have enriched my life, I particularly want to thank Janie Tankard, who stuck her neck out for me when it was neither popular nor easy to do so, and Sarah Meier, whose friendship has been a great blessing.

Lastly, I want to thank Daniel Negreanu, all of the supporters of The Reformation Project, and everyone who has offered me your support over the past several years in particular. There is no way I would be where I am today without it, and I deeply appreciate the sacrifices and contributions that so many have made to support both me and other LGBT Christians.

Notes

Introduction

1. Melissa Steffan, "Alan Chambers Apologizes to Gay Community, Exodus International to Shut Down," Gleanings, *Christianity Today,* June 21, 2013, www.christianitytoday.com/gleanings/2013 /june/alan-chambers-apologizes-to-gay-community-exodus.html.

Chapter 1

1. As Charles Hodge wrote in his *Systematic Theology,* "It is admitted that theologians are not infallible, in the interpretation of Scripture. It may, therefore, happen in the future, as it has in the past, that interpretations of the Bible, long confidently received, must be modified or abandoned, to bring revelation into harmony with what God teaches in his works. This change of view as to the true meaning of the Bible may be a painful trial to the Church, but it does not in the least impair the authority of the Scriptures. They remain infallible; we are merely convicted of having mistaken their meaning." Charles Hodge, *Systematic Theology* (London: Thomas Nelson and Sons, 1871), 1:59.

2. Albert Barnes wrote that "the word came to denote all who were religious teachers.... A false prophet is a teacher of incorrect doctrine, or one falsely and unjustly laying claims to divine inspiration." Likewise, Adam Clarke wrote, "By false prophets we are to understand *teachers* of erroneous doctrines," and John Gill explained that the phrase refers to "false teachers; for not such who pretended to foretell things to come, but such who set up themselves to be teachers of others, are here meant." Albert Barnes, *Notes, Explanatory and Practical, on the Gospels: Designed for Sunday School Teachers and Bible Classes,* 6th ed. (New York: Leavitt, Lord, & Co., 1835), 1:81; Adam Clarke, *The New Testament of Our Lord and Saviour Jesus Christ* (New York: J. Emory and B. Waugh,

1831), 1:82; and John Gill, *Gill's Exposition of the Entire Bible,*
"Matthew 7:15," Bible Hub, http://biblehub.com/matthew/7-15
.htm.

3. On the subject of slavery in Christian theology, see Mark A. Noll,
The Civil War as a Theological Crisis (Chapel Hill, NC: University
of North Carolina Press, 2006); Molly Oshatz, *Slavery and Sin:
The Fight against Slavery and the Rise of Liberal Protestantism* (New
York: Oxford University Press, 2012); Elizabeth Fox-Genovese and
Eugene D. Genovese, *The Mind of the Master Class: History and
Faith in the Southern Slaveholders' Worldview* (Cambridge: Cam-
bridge University Press, 2005); Jack Rogers, *Jesus, the Bible, and
Homosexuality: Explode the Myths, Heal the Church* (Louisville:
Westminster John Knox, 2009), 18–25, 32–33. For the history of
Christians' support for at least some forms of slavery, see Hector
Avalos, *Slavery, Abolitionism, and the Ethics of Biblical Scholarship*
(Sheffield, UK: Sheffield Phoenix, 2011), 159–225.

4. John M. G. Barclay, " 'Am I Not a Man and a Brother?' The Bible
and the British Anti-Slavery Campaign," *The Expository Times*
(October 2007): 119:3.

5. William Wilberforce, *An Appeal to the Religion, Justice, and Humanity of the Inhabitants of the British Empire, in Behalf of the Negro
Slaves in the West Indies* (London: J. Hatchard and Son, 1823), 13.

6. George B. Cheever, *The Guilt of Slavery and the Crime of Slavehold-
ing* (Boston: John P. Jewett, 1860), 462.

7. As New Testament scholar James Brownson wrote, "If same-sex
erotic acts are always morally wrong, then the impulse to engage in
those acts is also a manifestation of a disordered and sinful inner
state. Focusing on behavior alone—and regarding as neutral the
'preference' or inclination toward such behaviors—simply cannot
be justified from Scripture, particularly from the teachings of Jesus
in the Sermon on the Mount. If the acts are sinful, all inclinations
to such acts are to be understood as manifestations of a sinful
nature, and are to be resisted as such." James V. Brownson, *Bible,
Gender, Sexuality: Reframing the Church's Debate on Same-Sex
Relationships* (Grand Rapids, MI: Wm. B. Eerdmans, 2013), 175.

8. Brownson persuasively argued that the moral distinction between sexual orientation and sexual behavior made by many Christians who oppose same-sex relationships is "ultimately untenable.... Where does one draw the line? Where does the sinful impulse begin? Is it when gay or lesbian persons experience a desire for friendship with others of the same sex, admiration for another's physical beauty, the tendency to frequently think about another person, the persistent desire to be with another person, the desire to be touched by another, the desire to kiss or be kissed, or the desire for still more intimate contact? For most gay and lesbian persons, these desires are part of the same continuum, and they cannot always be readily distinguished from each other." Brownson, *Bible, Gender, Sexuality*, 175.

9. C. S. Lewis, *The Four Loves* (New York: Harcourt, Brace, 1960), 122.

10. According to the Family Acceptance Project, recent studies "have established a clear link between rejecting behaviors of families towards lesbian, gay and bisexual adolescents and negative health problems in early adulthood." "Publications," Family Acceptance Project, http://familyproject.sfsu.edu/publications. A 2009 paper in the journal *Pediatrics* showed that "lesbian, gay, and bisexual young adults who reported higher levels of family rejection during adolescence were 8.4 times more likely to report having attempted suicide, 5.9 times more likely to report high levels of depression, [and] 3.4 times more likely to use illegal drugs...compared with peers from families that reported no or low levels of family rejection." Caitlin Ryan, et al., "Family Rejection as a Predictor of Negative Health Outcomes in White and Latino Lesbian, Gay and Bisexual Young Adults," *Pediatrics*, 123, no. 1 (2009): 346–52.

Chapter 2

1. Maurice A. Finocchiaro, *The Galileo Affair: A Documentary History* (Berkeley: University of California Press, 1989), 28, 138.

2. Atle Naess, *Galileo Galilei: When the World Stood Still* (New York: Springer, 2004), 90.

3. Finocchiaro, *Galileo Affair*, 138.

4. Galileo Galilei, "Letter to the Grand Duchess Christina of Tuscany, 1615," Internet Modern History Sourcebook, Fordham University, August 1997, www.fordham.edu/halsall/mod/galileo-tuscany.asp.

5. Richard J. Blackwell, "The Bible at Galileo's Trial," in *Galileo, Bellarmine, and the Bible* (Notre Dame, IN: University of Notre Dame Press, 1992), 120.

6. As R. C. Sproul said, "Historically, the church's understanding of special revelation of the Bible has been corrected by students of natural revelation with the Copernican revolution." Keith Mathison, "Ligonier Ministries: The Teaching Fellowship of R.C. Sproul," May 25, 2012, www.ligonier.org/blog/interpreting-general-and-special-revelation-reformed-approach-science-and-scripture.

7. Similar terminology was used by the non-affirming author Stanley J. Grenz in his book *Welcoming but Not Affirming: An Evangelical Response to Homosexuality* (Louisville: Westminster John Knox Press, 1998).

8. Robert Gagnon wrote, "In sum, the Bible presents the anatomical, sexual, and procreative complementarity of male and female as clear and convincing proof of God's will for sexual unions," Robert A. J. Gagnon, *The Bible and Homosexual Practice: Texts and Hermeneutics* (Nashville: Abingdon, 2001), 37. So, too, James Hanigan wrote that the unity "enacted in sexual behavior…has its created basis in the physical and biological complementarity of male and female," James Hanigan, *Homosexuality: The Test Case for Christian Sexual Ethics* (Mahwah, NJ: Paulist Press, 1988), 101–2. The best analysis of varying understandings of gender complementarity is found in James Brownson's book *Bible, Gender, Sexuality: Reframing the Church's Debate on Same-Sex Relationships* (Grand Rapids, MI: Wm. B. Eerdmans, 2013), 16–38.

9. See John Piper and Wayne Grudem, eds., *Recovering Biblical Manhood and Womanhood: A Response to Evangelical Feminism* (Wheaton, IL: Crossway Books, 2006).

10. Gagnon is a prime example. He argues in detail that "the 'parts fit' male to female only" and that the Bible's statements about same-

sex behavior are grounded centrally in the "anatomical fittedness of the male penis and the female vagina." Gagnon, *The Bible and Homosexual Practice*, 63n54, 169. Grenz also argues that the "vagina and penis" are what "most readily allow male and female to complement the other," *Welcoming but Not Affirming*, 110. For more writings from non-affirming Christians who also support equal roles for men and women, see Ronald W. Pierce, Rebecca Merrill Groothuis, and Gordon D. Fee, eds., *Discovering Biblical Equality: Complementarity Without Hierarchy* (Downers Grove, IL: InterVarsity, 2005).

11. Robert A. J. Gagnon, "Robert Gagnon's Answers to Emails on the Bible and Homosexuality: The Fossil Canard," September 29, 2011, www.robgagnon.net/AnswersToEMails.htm.

12. Gagnon builds his entire sexual ethic around the criterion of "sameness." Elsewhere, he wrote, "The problem with same-sex intercourse is that it involves two noncomplementary sexual sames or likes. Similarly, incest is sex between familial sames or likes.... Scripture avoids the twin extremes of too much structural identity between sex partners (same-sex intercourse, incest) and too little (bestiality, sex with prepubescent children)." Dan O. Via and Robert A. J. Gagnon, *Homosexuality and the Bible: Two Views* (Minneapolis: Augsburg Fortress, 2003), 48. Gagnon is careful to argue that "anatomical fittedness" is not the only basis for gender complementarity, and at various points in his writings, he has pointed to many different factors he believes contribute to complementarity: "anatomy, procreation, sexual stimulation, relational expectations, and other gender differences that we today characterize with the slogan 'men are from Mars and women are from Venus.'" Via and Gagnon, *Homosexuality and the Bible*, 65. But male and female anatomy represents the core of Gagnon's argument about complementarity. As he wrote about Romans 1, "The appeal to nature in 1:26–27 has to do, at least primarily, with the visual perception of male-female bodily complementarity (the fittedness of the sex organs)." Gagnon, *The Bible and Homosexual Practice*, 257.

13. For more on this perspective, see Richard B. Hays, *The Moral Vision of the New Testament: A Contemporary Introduction to New*

Testament Ethics (San Francisco: HarperSanFrancisco, 1996) and "Relations Natural and Unnatural: A Response to John Boswell's Exegesis of Romans 1," *Journal of Religious Ethics* 14, no. 1 (1986). William Webb argued that "the deepest issue for the biblical authors was the breaking of sexual boundaries between male and female," which, in his view, makes the differences between ancient and modern same-sex practices of secondary importance for Christians. William J. Webb, *Slaves, Women and Homosexuals: Exploring the Hermeneutics of Cultural Analysis* (Downers Grove, IL: InterVarsity, 2001), 251.

14. Professional health organizations that oppose attempts to change individuals' sexual orientation include the American Psychological Association, the American Psychiatric Association, and the American Academy of Pediatrics. For reference, see "Expert Affidavit of Gregory M. Herek, PhD," GLAD, November 13, 2009, www.glad.org/uploads/docs/cases/gill-v-office-of-personnel-management/2009-11-17-doma-aff-herek.pdf.

15. Warren Throckmorton, "Alan Chambers: 99.9% have not experienced a change in their orientation," Patheos, January 9, 2012, www.patheos.com/blogs/warrenthrockmorton/2012/01/09/alan-chambers-99-9-have-not-experienced-a-change-in-their-orientation.

16. If you have doubts about the permanence of same-sex orientation, I strongly encourage you to read my friend Justin Lee's excellent book *Torn: Rescuing the Gospel from the Gays-vs.-Christians Debate* (New York: Jericho Books, 2013). Another helpful book for understanding same-sex orientation (although I disagree with the author's theological stance) is *Washed and Waiting: Reflections on Christian Faithfulness and Homosexuality* by Wesley Hill (Grand Rapids, MI: Zondervan, 2010). For more on the fixed nature of sexual orientation, see "Expert Affidavit," www.glad.org/uploads/docs/cases/gill-v-office-of-personnel-management/2009-11-17-doma-aff-herek.pdf, 12.

17. Stephen Long, "Falling in Love," *Sacred Tension* (blog), October 7, 2013, http://sacredtension.com/2013/10/07/falling-in-love/.

18. Hays, *Moral Vision*, 401.

19. As the historian Robert Padgug wrote, for many ancient societies, "sexual passion in any form implied sexual passion in all forms." Robert A. Padgug, "Sexual Matters: Rethinking Sexuality in History," *Radical History Review*, no. 20 (1979): 55.

20. Plato, *Laws*, 840a, trans. K. J. Dover, *Greek Homosexuality* (Cambridge, MA: Harvard University Press, 1989), 65.

21. Kallimakhos 11, *The Greek Anthology*, ed. A. S. F. Gow and Denys Page, i: *Hellenistic Epigrams* (Cambridge: Cambridge University Press, 1965). Quoted in Dover, *Greek Homosexuality*, 65.

22. Theokritos 2.44–45, quoted in Dover, *Greek Homosexuality*, 67.

23. *P. Tebtunis* 1.104, trans. A. S. Hunt and C. C. Edgar, in *Women's Life in Greece and Rome*, ed. Mary Lefkowitz and Maureen B. Fant (Baltimore: Johns Hopkins University Press, 1982), 59–60. Quoted in David M. Halperin, *One Hundred Years of Homosexuality: And Other Essays on Greek Love* (New York: Routledge, 1990), 34. For more examples of the ubiquity of bisexual attraction in ancient literature, see Dover, *Greek Homosexuality*, 63–67; and Craig A. Williams, *Roman Homosexuality*, 2nd ed. (Oxford: Oxford University Press, 2010), 17–66.

24. Plutarch, "The Dialogue on Love," 767, in *Moralia*, vol. 9, trans. Edwin L. Minar Jr. (London: Heinemann, 1961), 415.

25. For a more detailed exposition of this analogy, see Halperin, *One Hundred Years*, 26–27.

26. In addition to Halperin, see Dale B. Martin, "Heterosexism and the Interpretation of Romans 1:18–32," in *Sex and the Single Savior: Gender and Sexuality in Biblical Interpretation* (Louisville: Westminster John Knox, 2006), 51–64.

27. Dover, *Greek Homosexuality*, 65. See also Martti Nissinen, *Homoeroticism in the Biblical World: A Historical Perspective* (Minneapolis: Augsburg Fortress, 2004), 57–69; Kirk Ormand, *Controlling Desires: Sexuality in Ancient Greece and Rome*, Praeger Series on the Ancient World (Santa Barbara: Praeger, 2008), 56–58, 73–74, 117–22; and Marilyn B. Skinner, *Sexuality in Greek and Roman Culture* (Malden, MA: Blackwell, 2005), 62–71, 118–24.

28. Seneca, "On Master and Slave," *Moral Epistles,* 46, quoted by Victor Paul Furnish, "The Bible and Homosexuality," in Jeffrey S. Siker, ed., *Homosexuality in the Church: Both Sides of the Debate* (Louisville: Westminster John Knox, 1994), 26.

29. Cicero, *Philippicae,* 2.45, quoted in Williams, *Roman Homosexuality,* 38.

30. Polybius, 31.25.5, quoted in Williams, *Roman Homosexuality,* 71.

31. Cicero, *Philippicae,* 3.31, quoted in Williams, *Roman Homosexuality,* 112.

32. Nissinen, *Homoeroticism,* 19; Richard Elliott Friedman and Shawna Dolansky, *The Bible Now* (Oxford: Oxford University Press, 2011), 31–32; David F. Greenberg, *The Construction of Homosexuality* (Chicago: The University of Chicago Press, 1988), 131–32, 135.

33. Nissinen, *Homoeroticism,* 20–23.

34. Plutarch, "The Dialogue on Love," *On Love, the Family, and the Good Life: Selected Essays of Plutarch,* trans. Moses Hadas (New York: New American Library, 1957), 17.

35. Halperin, *One Hundred Years,* 31. "What Paul Veyne has said about the Romans can apply equally well to the classical Athenians: they were indeed puritans when it came to sex, but (unlike modern bourgeois Westerners) they were not puritans about conjugality and reproduction; rather, like many Mediterranean peoples, they were puritans about virility."

36. Plutarch, *Moralia,* 768E, quoted in Friedman and Dolansky, *Bible Now,* 34. Similarly strict attitudes existed throughout much of the ancient Near East, as Martti Nissinen has documented. See Nissinen, *Homoeroticism,* 19–36.

37. Aristotle, *Generation of Animals,* trans. A. L. Peck (Cambridge, MA: Loeb Classical Library, 1943), 175. Other sources that detail degrading views of women in the ancient world include Prudence Allen, *The Concept of Woman: The Early Humanist Reformation, 1250–1500* (Grand Rapids, MI: Wm. B. Eerdmans, 2002), 1:95–103; Simone de Beauvoir, *The Second Sex* (New York: Vintage Books, 1952), 61–96; and Peter Brown, "Body and City,"

in *The Body and Society: Men, Women, and Sexual Renunciation in Early Christianity* (New York: Columbia University Press, 1988), 9–17, 30.

38. Christine Garside Allen, "Plato on Women," *Feminist Studies* 2, no. 2/3 (1975): 131–38, www.jstor.org/stable/3177773. See also Plato, *Timaeus,* trans. Benjamin Jowett, 2009, http://classics.mit.edu /Plato/timaeus.html.

39. Halperin analyzed a translation of a second-century AD work about men who take the passive role in same-sex relations. He wrote, "Their affliction is not natural (that is, organic) but is rather their own excessive desire.... They turn to receptive sex because, although they try, they are not able to satisfy themselves by means of more conventionally masculine sorts of sexual activity, including insertive sex with women; far from having desires that are structured differently from those of normal folk, these gender-deviants desire sexual pleasure just as most people do, but they have such strong and intense desires that they are driven to devise some unusual and disreputable (though ultimately futile) means of gratifying them." David Halperin, *One Hundred Years of Homosexuality,* 22–23.

40. Diogenes Laertius, *Lives of Eminent Philosophers,* 7.110, quoted by David E. Fredrickson, "Natural and Unnatural Use in Romans 1:24–27: Paul and the Philosophic Critique of Eros," in *Homosexuality, Science, and the "Plain Sense" of Scripture,* ed. David L. Balch (Grand Rapids, MI: Wm. B. Eerdmans, 2000), 206.

41. Plato, *Laws,* 636b–d, quoted in Thomas K. Hubbard, ed., *Homosexuality in Greece and Rome: A Sourcebook of Basic Documents* (Berkeley: University of California Press, 2003), 252.

42. Musonius Rufus, "On Sexual Matters," quoted in Hubbard, *Homosexuality,* 394–95.

43. Hays, "Relations Natural and Unnatural," 200. Mark Smith, a non-affirming scholar, also acknowledged that "the modern concept of an inherent sexual orientation" is "something no ancient Greek or Roman was familiar with." Mark D. Smith, "Ancient Bisexuality and the Interpretation of Romans 1:26–27," *Journal of*

the American Academy of Religion 64, no. 2 (1996), 225. Marion Soards, another non-affirming scholar, wrote that "neither Paul nor any other ancient person had a concept of 'sexual orientation.'" Marion Soards, *Scripture & Homosexuality: Biblical Authority and the Church Today* (Louisville: Westminster John Knox, 1995), 22. Jenell Williams Paris, who is also non-affirming, has written that "contemporary categories for sexuality weren't present in biblical cultures or even in my own society just over a hundred years ago." Jenell Williams Paris, *The End of Sexual Identity: Why Sex Is Too Important to Define Who We Are* (Downers Grove, IL: IVP Books, 2011), 8–9.

44. John Chrysostom, *Homily 4 on Romans,* trans. J. Walker, J. Sheppard, and H. Browne, rev. George B. Stevens, in *Nicene and Post-Nicene Fathers,* 1st ser., vol. 11, ed. Philip Schaff (Buffalo, NY: Christian Literature Publishing, 1889), at New Advent, rev. and ed. Kevin Knight, www.newadvent.org/fathers/210204.htm.

45. Michael Rocke, *Forbidden Friendships: Homosexuality and Male Culture in Renaissance Florence* (New York: Oxford University Press, 1998), 162. See also Francis Mark Mondimore, *A Natural History of Homosexuality* (Baltimore: Johns Hopkins University Press, 1996), 23.

46. Jeffrey Weeks, *Coming Out: Homosexual Politics in Britain from the Nineteenth Century to the Present* (London: Quartet Books, 1979), 12. See also Padgug, "Sexual Matters," 12.

47. Halperin, *One Hundred Years,* 15; Mondimore, *A Natural History of Homosexuality,* 34–51.

48. In Plato's *Symposium,* for instance, Aristophanes relates a myth explaining the existence of three types of people: adulterers and adulteresses, men who exclusively pursue boys and continue to live with them after they mature, and women who actively seek other women. But as Kirk Ormand has argued in *Controlling Desires,* this comic speech is not describing what is normal and expected, but what is deviant and transgressive: "None of the so-called orientations described previously are exactly like ours, and more important, none of them would be considered normal by Plato's

Athenian audience. Each of them is a type of excess, and the story turns out to be not about how to produce gay or straight men and women, but how certain kinds of odd and excessive preferences came to be. When describing those preferences, Aristophanes still assumes a pederastic model for the male-male couple. The category of homosexual male, in which two men of the same age would be attracted to each other, and either at any given time could be thought of as lover or beloved, simply seems not to be thinkable." Ormand, *Controlling Desires*, 98. Similar analyses can be found in Halperin, *One Hundred Years*, 18–21; Skinner, *Sexuality in Greek and Roman Culture*, 129–32; and Jeffrey S. Carnes, "This Myth Which Is Not One: Construction of Discourse in Plato's *Symposium*," in *Rethinking Sexuality: Foucault and Classical Antiquity*, ed. David H. J. Larmour, Paul Allen Miller, and Charles Platter (Princeton, NJ: Princeton University Press, 1998), 104–21.

Chapter 3

1. Gay Christians could theoretically marry a person of the opposite sex despite their sexual orientation. But as Jim Brownson has written, "Encouraging heterosexual marriage in such cases is fraught with peril.... Already, many marriages fail because one partner finally acknowledges that his or her sexual orientation is not compatible with heterosexual marriage. Encouraging marriages that are likely to end in divorce is not Christian faithfulness." James V. Brownson, *Bible, Gender, Sexuality: Reframing the Church's Debate on Same-Sex Relationships* (Grand Rapids, MI: Wm. B. Eerdmans, 2013), 143.
2. Genesis 1:9–10, 12, 18, 21, 25.
3. See Brownson's discussion in *Bible, Gender, Sexuality*, 29–31. He wrote, "The primary movement in the text is not from unity to differentiation, but from the isolation of an individual to the deep blessing of shared kinship and community.... The text doesn't really explore gender differences at all; instead, it places the emphasis on the value of shared human experience between the man and the woman," 30–31.

4. John Paul II, *Man and Woman He Created Them: A Theology of the Body* (Boston: Pauline Books & Media, 2006), 160.
5. Anthony A. Hoekema, *Created in God's Image* (Grand Rapids, MI: Wm. B. Eerdmans, 1994), 77. See also William Stacy Johnson, *A Time to Embrace: Same-Gender Relationships in Religion, Law, and Politics* (Grand Rapids, MI: Wm. B. Eerdmans, 2006), 122–26. The word "helper" is used of God elsewhere in the Old Testament, so it does not necessarily imply inferiority (see Exodus 18:4; Deuteronomy 33:7, 26, 29; Psalm 33:20; and 115:9–11). On this subject, see M. L. Rosenzweig, "A Helper Equal to Him," *Judaism* 139 (1986).
6. For a helpful discussion of the figure of the eunuch in Matthew 19:11–12, see Barry Danylak, *Redeeming Singleness* (Wheaton, IL: Crossway, 2010), 150–63.
7. Stephen Long, "Falling in Love," *Sacred Tension* (blog), October 7, 2013, http://sacredtension.com/2013/10/07/falling-in-love/.
8. See Elizabeth A. Clark, *Reading Renunciation: Asceticism and Scripture in Early Christianity* (Princeton, NJ: Princeton University Press, 1999); Christine A. Colón and Bonnie E. Field, *Singled Out: Why Celibacy Must Be Reinvented in Today's Church* (Grand Rapids, MI: BrazosPress, 2009), 189–94; and Dale B. Martin, "Familiar Idolatry and the Christian Case Against Marriage," *Sex and the Single Savior: Gender and Sexuality in Biblical Interpretation* (Louisville: Westminster John Knox, 2006), 103–24.
9. Peter Brown, *The Body and Society: Men, Women, and Sexual Renunciation in Early Christianity* (New York: Columbia University Press, 1988), 88.
10. Brown, *Body and Society,* 92.
11. Brown, *Body and Society,* 116.
12. See Irenaeus, *Against Heresies,* 5 vols. (Oxford: J. Parker, 1872). For some of the difficulties involved in discussing Gnosticism, see Karen L. King, *What Is Gnosticism?* (Cambridge, MA: Harvard University Press, 2005); and Ismo Dunderberg, *Beyond Gnosticism: Myth, Lifestyle, and Society in the School of Valentinus* (New York: Columbia University Press, 2008).

13. Brown, *The Body and Society,* 86. John Chrysostom named the Manicheans, the Encratites, and the Marcionites as those under condemnation in 1 Timothy 4. John Chrysostom, *Homily 12 on First Timothy,* in *Nicene and Post-Nicene Fathers,* 1st ser., vol. 13, ed. and trans. Philip Schaff (Buffalo, NY: Christian Literature Publishing, 1889), at New Advent, rev. and ed. Kevin Knight, www.newadvent.org/fathers/230612.htm.

14. Tertullian, *Against Marcion,* bk. 1, trans. Peter Holmes, in *Ante-Nicene Fathers,* vol. 3, ed. Alexander Roberts, James Donaldson, and A. Cleveland Coxe (Buffalo, NY: Christian Literature Publishing, 1885), at New Advent, rev. and ed. Kevin Knight, www.newadvent.org/fathers/03121.htm.

15. Tertullian, *Prescription Against Heretics,* trans. Peter Holmes, in *Ante-Nicene Fathers,* vol. 3, ed. Alexander Roberts, James Donaldson, and A. Cleveland Coxe (Buffalo, NY: Christian Literature Publishing, 1885), at New Advent, rev. and ed. Kevin Knight, www.newadvent.org/fathers/0311.htm.

16. Irenaeus, *Against Heresies,* bk. 1, trans. Alexander Roberts and William Rambaut, in *Ante-Nicene Fathers,* vol. 1, ed. Alexander Roberts, James Donaldson, and A. Cleveland Coxe (Buffalo, NY: Christian Literature Publishing, 1885), at New Advent, rev. and ed. Kevin Knight, www.newadvent.org/fathers/0103128.htm.

17. Jerome, *Against Jovinianus,* bk. 2, trans. W. H. Fremantle, G. Lewis, and W. G. Martley, in *Nicene and Post-Nicene Fathers,* 2nd ser., vol. 6, ed. Philip Schaff and Henry Wace (Buffalo, NY: Christian Literature Publishing, 1893), at New Advent, rev. and ed. Kevin Knight, www.newadvent.org/fathers/30092.htm.

18. Jerome, *Letter 48: To Pammachius,* trans. W. H. Fremantle, G. Lewis, and W. G. Martley, in *Nicene and Post-Nicene Fathers,* 2nd ser., vol. 6, ed. Philip Schaff and Henry Wace (Buffalo, NY: Christian Literature Publishing, 1893), at New Advent, rev. and ed. Kevin Knight, www.newadvent.org/fathers/3001048.htm.

19. Augustine, *Contra Faustum,* bk. 30, trans. Richard Stothert, in *Nicene and Post-Nicene Fathers,* 1st ser., vol. 4, ed. Philip Schaff (Buffalo, NY: Christian Literature Publishing, 1887), at New

Advent, rev. and ed. Kevin Knight, www.newadvent.org/fathers
/140630.htm.

20. See Athanasius, *On the Incarnation* (Crestwood, NY: St. Vladimir's
Seminary Press, 1993). See also Augustine, *The City of God,* bk.
10, trans. Marcus Dods, in *Nicene and Post-Nicene Fathers,* 1st ser.,
vol. 2, ed. Philip Schaff (Buffalo, NY: Christian Literature Publishing, 1887), at New Advent, rev. and ed. Kevin Knight, www.new
advent.org/fathers/120110.htm.

21. Bertrand Russell, *A History of Western Philosophy* (New York:
Simon & Schuster/Touchstone, 1967), 134–42.

22. Seneca, *Letters from a Stoic: Epistulae Morales Ad Lucilium,* 65.16,
trans. Robin Campbell (Harmondsworth, UK: Penguin, 1969).

23. See N. T. Wright's discussion of dualism and types of duality in
The New Testament and the People of God, Christian Origins and
the Question of God, vol. 1 (Minneapolis: Fortress, 1992),
252–56.

24. See N. T. Wright, *Surprised by Hope: Rethinking Heaven, the
Resurrection, and the Mission of the Church* (New York: HarperOne,
2008).

25. Augustine, *Of Holy Virginity,* trans. C. L. Cornish, in *Nicene and
Post-Nicene Fathers,* 1st ser., vol. 3, ed. Philip Schaff (Buffalo, NY:
Christian Literature Publishing, 1887), at New Advent, rev. and
ed. Kevin Knight, www.newadvent.org/fathers/1310.htm.

26. Ambrose, *Concerning Virginity,* bk. 1, trans. H. de Romestin,
E. de Romestin, and H. T. F. Duckworth, in *Nicene and Post-
Nicene Fathers,* 2nd ser., vol. 10, ed. Philip Schaff and Henry
Wace (Buffalo, NY: Christian Literature Publishing, 1896), at
New Advent, rev. and ed. Kevin Knight, www.newadvent.org
/fathers/34071.htm.

27. John Calvin, *Matthew, Mark and Luke,* pt. 2, Calvin's Commentaries, vol. 32, trans. John King (1847–50), at Internet Sacred
Text Archive, www.sacred-texts.com/chr/calvin/cc32/cc32069
.htm.

28. John Calvin, *Institutes of the Christian Religion,* trans. Henry
Beveridge (Peabody, MA: Hendrickson, 2009), 257–58.

29. Calvin, *Institutes,* 258.
30. Calvin, *Institutes,* 841.
31. Martin Luther, "Judgement of Martin Luther on Monastic Vows" (1521/22), in *The Christian in Society I,* ed. James Atkinson, Luther's Works, vol. 44, (Philadelphia: Fortress, 1966), 262. Quoted in Christopher C. Roberts, *Creation and Covenant: The Significance of Sexual Difference in the Moral Theology of Marriage* (New York: T & T Clark, 2007), 117.
32. John Paul II, *Man and Woman,* 416.
33. John Paul II, *Man and Woman,* 414.
34. According to John Paul II, marriage and celibacy thus "explain or complete each other." John Paul II, *Man and Woman,* 430. For more on this idea, see Christopher West, *Theology of the Body for Beginners: A Basic Introduction to Pope John Paul II's Sexual Revolution* (West Chester, PA: Ascension, 2004), 65–76. In reference to John Paul II's views on celibacy, West wrote, "If someone were to choose this vocation based on a fear or rejection of sex, or because of deep-seated sexual wounds that prevented a healthy married life, it would not correspond to Christ's invitation," 73.
35. Karl Barth, *Church Dogmatics,* vol. 3, pt. 4 (London: T & T Clark, 2004), 146.
36. Protestant theologian Barry Danylak wrote of "the positive vision the Christian Scriptures provide for *both* marriage and singleness as well as for human sexuality: Christian marriage is a testimony of the utterly faithful and unchanging love of God for his people in a permanent covenant relationship with him; Christian singleness is a testimony to the complete sufficiency of Christ for the present age and gives visible witness to the hope of our eternal inheritance yet to come; and Christian sexuality is an expression of the exclusive unity and oneness in the bond of the marriage relationship." Danylak, *Redeeming Singleness,* 214.

Chapter 4

1. Genesis 10:19 mentions Sodom and Gomorrah, but does not discuss the people who live there.

2. John Calvin, *Commentary on Genesis,* vol. 1, Christian Classics Ethereal Library, last modified July 13, 2005, www.ccel.org/ccel /calvin/calcom01.xxiv.i.html.

3. See Deuteronomy 29:23; 32:32; Isaiah 1:9–10; 3:9; 13:19; Jeremiah 20:16; 23:14; 49:18; 50:40; Lamentations 4:6; Ezekiel 16:46–56; Amos 4:1–11; Zephaniah 2:8–11.

4. The term translated as "detestable things" (*toevah*) is used 117 times in the Old Testament. Only two of those references, Leviticus 18:22 and 20:13, refer to male same-sex intercourse. The term *toevah* appears forty other times in the book of Ezekiel, mostly to describe idolatrous practices. (See, for example, Ezekiel 8:9–10.) In the immediate context of Ezekiel 16, the word *toevah* refers to idolatry and adultery (verses 2, 22, 36, 43, 47, 51, and 58), not to same-sex behavior. So it's contextually unlikely that Ezekiel's reference to "detestable things" in verse 50 represents a condemnation of same-sex behavior. And even if one *does* interpret the term in that sense, the only form of same-sex behavior mentioned in Genesis 19 is a threatened gang rape—not committed, consensual relationships.

5. See Michael Carden, *Sodomy: A History of a Christian Biblical Myth* (London: Equinox, 2004), 42–78.

6. All three quotes from NRSV. Sirach and Wisdom are understood as deuterocanonical by Roman Catholics, while 3 Maccabees is included in the canon of Greek and Russian Orthodox Christians. Only two Jewish texts before the time of Christ directly link Sodom's sin to sexual transgressions. But even these works, *Testaments of the Twelve Patriarchs* and *Jubilees* (second century BC), focus on sexual sins in general, not same-sex behavior in particular. See Carden, *Sodomy,* 52.

7. For ancient texts describing this understanding of same-sex rape, see Martti Nissinen, *Homoeroticism in the Biblical World: A Historical Perspective* (Minneapolis: Augsburg Fortress, 2004), 48–49.

8. See Christine D. Pohl, *Making Room: Recovering Hospitality as a Christian Tradition* (Grand Rapids, MI: Wm. B. Eerdmans, 1999), 28. See also John Boswell, *Christianity, Social Tolerance, and*

Homosexuality: Gay People in Western Europe from the Beginning of the Christian Era to the Fourteenth Century (Chicago: University of Chicago Press, 1980), 96.

9. Pohl, *Making Room,* 25–28. See also T. Desmond Alexander, "Lot's Hospitality: A Clue to His Righteousness," *Journal of Biblical Literature* 104 (1985): 289–91.

10. In Judges 19:1–10, the concubine's father welcomes the Levite into his home for several days.

11. For more on some modern Christians' views on gender hierarchy, see John Piper, "Manhood and Womanhood Before Sin," Desiring God, May 28, 1989, www.desiringgod.org/resource-library/sermons /manhood-and-womanhood-before-sin. Piper wrote that men and women "are to enjoy equality of personhood, equality of dignity, mutual respect, harmony, complementarity, and a unified destiny."

12. In Matthew 11:23–24, Jesus invoked Sodom as a symbol of unrepentance. In Luke 17:28–29, he said that the people of Sodom "were eating and drinking, buying and selling, planting and building" before their destruction. He was not condemning those activities, but underscoring the unexpected nature of "the day the Son of Man is revealed" (verse 30). Other New Testament references to Sodom are found in Romans 9:29 and Revelation 11:8.

13. The New International Version of the Bible translates the phrase even more broadly, as "the depraved conduct of the lawless."

14. See Carden, *Sodomy,* 62. See also Nissinen, *Homoeroticism,* 92. Robert Gagnon acknowledged that the phrase "strange flesh" most likely refers to angels, but he argued that the term translated as "gross immorality" (*ekporneusasai*) should be taken as a condemnation of same-sex behavior. But that interpretation is based on conjecture. *Ekporneusasai* describes sexual immorality in general, not same-sex behavior in particular. Robert A. J. Gagnon *The Bible and Homosexual Practice: Texts and Hermeneutics* (Nashville: Abingdon, 2002), 87–88.

15. Philo, *On Abraham,* trans. F. H. Colson (Cambridge, MA: Harvard University Press, 1954), 133–41, www.well.com/~aquarius/philo -abraham.htm.

16. Origen, *Homilies on Genesis and Exodus* (Washington, DC: Catholic University of America Press, 2002), 112.

17. See Carden, *Sodomy,* 139–41.

18. John Cassian, *Institutes,* 5.6, quoted in Carden, *Sodomy,* 125.

19. John Chrysostom, *Homily 8 on First Thessalonians,* trans. John A. Broadus, in *Nicene and Post-Nicene Fathers,* 1st ser., vol. 13, ed. Philip Schaff (Buffalo, NY: Christian Literature Publishing, 1889), at New Advent, rev. and ed. Kevin Knight, www.newadvent.org /fathers/230408.htm.

20. Paulus Orosius, *The Seven Books of History against the Pagans,* trans. R. J. Deferrari (Washington, DC: Catholic University of America Press), 1.5. Quoted in Carden, *Sodomy,* 125. Carden said of similar writings, "What is striking, in reading these texts, is that homosexual behavior is not seen as aberrant or deviant but as a potentiality within everyone. It arises when people give themselves over to rich indulgent living, something with which Sodom is already primarily associated, and the resulting excessive pleasure and passion," 124.

21. Augustine, "To Consentius: Against Lying," in *Nicene and Post-Nicene Fathers,* 1st ser., vol. 3, ed. Philip Schaff, trans. H. Browne (Buffalo, NY: Christian Literature Publishing, 1887), 497.

22. *Levir* is the Latin term for "husband's brother."

23. For more on the history of interpretation of Genesis 38, see John T. Noonan, Jr., *Contraception: A History of Its Treatment by the Catholic Theologians and Canonists* (Cambridge, MA: The Belknap Press of Harvard University Press, 1965), 34–36, 49–55, 527–28; Elizabeth A. Clark, *Reading Renunciation: Asceticism and Scripture in Early Christianity* (New York: Columbia University Press, 1988), 290–91. Clark wrote, "Here we have an excellent example of how a Biblical verse, when transported to a different venue in which its original referents were inapplicable (here, an all-male monastery), could be adapted to fit the new situation."

24. See Mark D. Jordan, *The Ethics of Sex* (Malden, MA: Blackwell, 2002), 95–104. See also *Onania; or, The Heinous Sin of Self-Pollution, and All Its Frightful Consequences in Both Sexes* (1723), http://books.google.com/books?id=O6Q_AAAAcAAJ.

25. For more on the development of the category of "sodomy" in Christian theology, see Mark D. Jordan, *The Invention of Sodomy in Christian Theology* (Chicago: University of Chicago Press, 1997).

Chapter 5

1. Paul summed up this idea in Galatians 3:23–25, writing, "Before the coming of this faith, we were held in custody under the law, locked up until the faith that was to come would be revealed. So the law was our guardian until Christ came that we might be justified by faith. Now that this faith has come, we are no longer under a guardian." The law was good, Paul wrote, and its purpose vital. But its purpose was also temporary. Once Christ fulfilled the law, his followers would have trivialized his sacrifice by living as though they were still subject to the law's constraints. Paul wrote in Galatians 5:2 that Christ "will be of no value to you at all" if you continue to live as a slave to the law.

2. The prohibitions of incest, adultery, and bestiality in Leviticus 18 and 20 are repeated multiple times in the rest of the Old Testament, *unlike* the prohibition of male same-sex relations. Incest is prohibited in Deuteronomy 22:30 and 27:20–23. Adultery is prohibited in Exodus 20:14; Deuteronomy 5:18 and 22:22–27; Numbers 5:11–31; and Ezekiel 18:6–11 and 33:26. Bestiality is prohibited in Exodus 22:19 and Deuteronomy 27:21. But it's an open question whether even the incest prohibitions are absolute. After all, although Leviticus 18:16 forbids a man from having sexual relations with his brother's wife, Deuteronomy 25:5–6 commands this practice when a man dies without a son. Barry Danylak, among other commentators, interprets Deuteronomy 25 as an "exception clause" to the incest prohibitions of Leviticus. Barry Danylak, *Redeeming Singleness: How the Storyline of Scripture Affirms the Single Life* (Wheaton, IL: Crossway Books, 2010), 69.

3. *For the Bible Tells Me So,* directed by Daniel G. Karslake (Atticus Group, 2007).

4. Phyllis A. Bird, "The Bible in Christian Ethical Deliberation Concerning Homosexuality: Old Testament Contributions," in *Homosexuality, Science, and the "Plain Sense" of Scripture,* ed. David L. Balch (Grand Rapids, MI: Wm. B. Eerdmans, 2000), 152.

5. Saul M. Olyan, "'And with a Male You Shall Not Lie the Lying Down of a Woman': On the Meaning and Significance of Leviticus 18:22 and 20:13," *Journal of the History of Sexuality* 5, no. 2 (1994): 180; Daniel Boyarin, "Are There Any Jews in 'The History of Sexuality'?" *Journal of the History of Sexuality* 5, no. 3 (1995): 334; and Michael L. Satlow, "They Abused Him Like a Woman," *Journal of the History of Sexuality* 5, no. 1 (1994). See also Jay Michaelson, *God vs. Gay?: The Religious Case for Equality* (Boston: Beacon Press, 2011), 62–64; "Does the Bible Really Call Homosexuality an 'Abomination'?" *Religion Dispatches,* July 1, 2010, www.religiondispatches.org/archive/sexandgender/2826 /does_the_bible_really_call_homosexuality_an_"abomination".

6. See Jack Rogers, *Jesus, the Bible, and Homosexuality: Explode the Myths, Heal the Church* (Louisville: Westminster John Knox, 2009), 68.

7. Philo, *The Special Laws,* vol. 3, at Peter Kirby, "The Works of Philo," Early Christian Writings, 2013, www.earlychristianwritings .com/yonge/book29.html.

8. Plutarch, *Dialogue on Love,* 751d, quoted by Victor Paul Furnish, "The Bible and Homosexuality: Reading the Texts in Context," in Jeffrey S. Siker, ed., *Homosexuality in the Church: Both Sides of the Debate* (Louisville: Westminster John Knox, 1994), 27.

9. Clement of Alexandria, *The Instructor,* The Paedagogus, bk. 3, trans. Bernadette J. Brooten, in *Love Between Women: Early Christian Responses to Female Homoeroticism* (Chicago: University of Chicago Press, 1996), 324.

10. Clement of Alexandria, *The Instructor,* The Paedagogus, bk. 3, trans. William Wilson, in *Ante-Nicene Fathers,* vol. 2, ed. Alexander Roberts, James Donaldson, and A. Cleveland Coxe (Buffalo, NY: Christian Literature Publishing, 1885), at New Advent, rev. and ed. Kevin Knight, www.newadvent.org/fathers/02093.htm.

11. Olyan, "And with a Male," 183–86.

12. Boyarin, "Are There Any Jews," 336–39.

13. *Middle Assyrian Laws,* quoted in Martti Nissinen, *Homoeroticism in the Biblical World: A Historical Perspective* (Minneapolis: Augsburg Fortress, 2004), 25.

14. Nissinen, *Homoeroticism,* 27–28.

15. Richard Elliott Friedman and Shawna Dolansky, *The Bible Now* (Oxford: Oxford University Press, 2011), 35.

16. For extensive documentation of ancient condemnations of female same-sex relations, see Brooten, *Love Between Women.*

17. Pseudo-Lucian, *Erōtes* 28, M. D. Macleod, ed., *Luciani Opera,* vol. 3 (Oxford: Clarendon Press, 1980), 101. Cited by Brooten in *Love Between Women,* 54. Even when later Jewish rabbis sought to condemn female same-sex relations, they did not appeal to Leviticus 18:22 or 20:13. If those prohibitions had been understood to condemn all forms of same-sex behavior, the rabbis could have referred to them. See Brooten, *Love Between Women,* 64–65.

18. John Piper and Wayne Grudem, eds., *Recovering Biblical Manhood and Womanhood: A Response to Evangelical Feminism* (Wheaton, IL: Crossway Books, 2006), xv.

19. For more examples of the subordinate status of women in ancient Israel, see William J. Webb, *Slaves, Women and Homosexuals: Exploring the Hermeneutics of Cultural Analysis* (Downers Grove, IL: InterVarsity, 2001), 45–49.

20. As James Brownson wrote, Scripture's "overall movement...with respect to patriarchy is thus away from roles defined by household responsibilities in the ancient world—including the divisions of honor, status, and worth defined along gender lines—and toward a vision of mutuality and equality in which the procreative enterprise of male and female no longer defines human identity at its core." James V. Brownson, *Bible, Gender, Sexuality: Reframing the Church's Debate on Same-Sex Relationships* (Grand Rapids, MI: Wm. B. Eerdmans, 2013), 81.

21. John Piper, *This Momentary Marriage: A Parable of Permanence* (Wheaton, IL: Crossway Books, 2009), 160.

Chapter 6

1. *Prayers for Bobby,* directed by Russell Mulcahy (Daniel Sladek Entertainment, 2009).

2. *For the Bible Tells Me So,* directed by Daniel G. Karslake (Atticus Group, 2007).

3. See Willard M. Swartley, *Slavery, Sabbath, War, and Women: Case Issues in Biblical Interpretation* (Harrisonburg, VA: Herald, 1983); William J. Webb, *Slaves, Women and Homosexuals: Exploring the Hermeneutics of Cultural Analysis* (Downers Grove, IL: InterVarsity, 2001); and Mark Noll, *The Civil War as a Theological Crisis* (Chapel Hill, NC: University of North Carolina Press, 2006).

4. See Webb, *Slaves.*

5. For more on this idea, see Webb, *Slaves;* 105–6, 203–4; James V. Brownson, *Bible, Gender, Sexuality: Reframing the Church's Debate on Same-Sex Relationships* (Grand Rapids, MI: Wm. B. Eerdmans, 2013), 6; and Michael Philip Penn, *Kissing Christians: Ritual and Community in the Late Ancient Church* (Philadelphia: University of Pennsylvania Press, 2005).

6. Webb, *Slaves,* 216.

7. John Boswell, *Christianity, Social Tolerance, and Homosexuality: Gay People in Western Europe from the Beginning of the Christian Era to the Fourteenth Century* (Chicago: University of Chicago Press, 1980), 106–17. Boswell wrote, "It cannot be inferred from this that Paul considered mere homoerotic attraction or practice morally reprehensible, since the passage strongly implies that he was not discussing persons who were by inclination gay and since he carefully observed, in regard to both the women and the men, that they changed or abandoned the 'natural use' to engage in homosexual activities" (112–13).

8. Boswell, *Christianity,* 109.

9. Pseudo-Lucian, *Affairs of the Heart,* 22, quoted in Robert A. J. Gagnon, *The Bible and Homosexual Practice: Texts and Hermeneutics* (Nashville: Abingdon, 2002), 179n.

10. Plato, *Laws,* 839, quoted in Thomas K. Hubbard, ed., *Homosexuality in Greece and Rome: A Sourcebook of Basic Documents* (Berkeley: University of California Press, 2003), 256.

11. Dio Chrysostom, "The Seventh or Euboean Discourse," *Discourses,* vol. 1, at University of Chicago, last modified September 21, 2012, http://penelope.uchicago.edu/Thayer/E/Roman/Texts /Dio_Chrysostom/Discourses/7*.html.

12. Chrysostom, "The Seventh or Euboean Discourse."

13. John Chrysostom, *Homilies on Romans,* 4, quoted in Gerald Bray and Thomas C. Oden, eds., *Ancient Christian Commentary on Scripture: Romans,* New Testament vol. 6 (Downers Grove, IL: InterVarsity, 1998), 47–48.

14. Curtis M. Wong, "India's Gay Sex Law Praised by Bryan Fischer," Huffington Post, December 13, 2013, www.huffingtonpost. com/2013/12/13/india-gay-law-bryan-fischer_n_4439543.html.

15. "Discussion: Christianity and Homosexuality," YouTube video, 7:54, from the *Speaking of Faith* radio program, posted by "deep-coffee," May 12, 2008, www.youtube.com/watch?v=PkWk1ATY Hno.

16. Plato, *Laws,* 636b–d, quoted in Hubbard, *Homosexuality,* 252.

17. Plutarch, *Dialogue on Love,* 5, quoted in Hubbard, *Homosexuality,* 455.

18. Josephus, *Against Apion,* quoted in Richard B. Hays, "Relations Natural and Unnatural: A Response to John Boswell's Exegesis of Romans 1," *Journal of Religious Ethics* 14, no. 1 (1986): 193; and Bernadette J. Brooten, *Love Between Women: Early Christian Responses to Female Homoeroticism* (Chicago: University of Chicago Press, 1996), 245n86.

19. Philo, *On Abraham,* trans. F. H. Colson (Cambridge, MA: Harvard University Press, 1954), 133–41, www.well.com/~aquarius/philo -abraham.htm.

20. Philo, *On Abraham.*

21. *The Sentences of Pseudo-Phocylides,* quoted in Gagnon, *Bible and Homosexual Practice,* 171.

22. Pseudo-Lucian, *Amores; or Affairs of the Heart,* quoted in Gagnon, *Bible and Homosexual Practice,* 166n10.

23. James Miller argued that Romans 1:26 refers to "unnatural" heterosexual behavior in his essay "The Practices of Romans 1:26: Homosexual or Heterosexual?" *Novum Testamentum* 37 (1995),

1–11. James Brownson made the same case, noting that "both Clement of Alexandria and Augustine interpret Romans 1:26 as referring to oral or anal intercourse between women and men." Brownson, *Bible, Gender, Sexuality,* 207–8; see also 224–25. Bernadette Brooten, however, challenged Miller's reading of ancient sources on this point, arguing that "the type of sexual relations engaged in by women most often called 'contrary to nature' (para physin) in the Roman world is sexual relations between women." Brooten, *Love Between Women,* 248–53. I'm inclined to agree with Brooten's argument here, even though it isn't definitive. (As she noted, some Greek Stoics considered hetero-sexual adultery to be unnatural. *Love Between Women,* 251n101.) But ultimately, whether Romans 1:26 refers to female same-sex relations or to opposite-sex behavior doesn't alter my argument. The mere existence of the debate, however, further underscores the differences between ancient understandings of nature and the interpretations of many non-affirming Christians today.

24. See Gareth Moore, *A Question of Truth: Christianity and Homo-sexuality* (London: Continuum, 2003), 96–99. See also David E. Fredrickson's discussion of the lack of mutuality implied in the phrase "sexual use," "Natural and Unnatural Use in Romans 1:24–27: Paul and the Philosophic Critique of Eros," in *Homo-sexuality, Science, and the "Plain Sense" of Scripture,* ed. David L. Balch (Grand Rapids, MI: Wm. B. Eerdmans, 2000), 199–207.

25. Robert A. J. Gagnon, "Truncated Love: A Response to Andrew Marin's *Love Is an Orientation,*" pt. 1, August 31, 2010, www .robgagnon.net/articlesonline.htm.

26. Gagnon, *Bible and Homosexual Practice,* 291.

27. Gagnon has argued that, because the truth of God is visible in creation (Romans 1:19–20), God's will for human sexuality is also "visibly manifest in male and female bodies." Hence, Gagnon reads Romans 1:26–27 to indicate that, "along with idolatry, same-sex intercourse represents one of the clearest instances of conscious suppression of revelation in nature by gentiles, inasmuch as it involves denying clear anatomical gender differences and functions

(leaving them 'without excuse')." Gagnon, *Bible and Homosexual Practice*, 264–66. But as Brownson wrote, "This reading confuses Paul's meaning. What Paul actually says in these two verses is that what can be known about God is plain or visible in the creation, specifically God's eternal power and divine nature. The focus here is not on knowledge of human things, but on the knowledge of God.... It appears that the notion of 'anatomical gender complementarity' is really a modern concept rather than a category that actually shaped ethical thought about sex in the ancient world. To the extent that ancient references to 'nature' in sexual ethics envisioned anatomy and biology, they clearly had procreation in mind." Brownson, *Bible, Gender, Sexuality*, 241–43.

28. Helmut Koester, "Physis," ed. Gerhard Kittel and Gerhard Friedrich, *Theological Dictionary of the New Testament*, vol. 9 (Grand Rapids, MI: Wm. B. Eerdmans, 1977), 262. See also G. E. R. Lloyd, "The Invention of Nature," *Methods and Problems in Greek Science* (Cambridge: Cambridge University Press, 1991), 417–34.

29. Euripides, *The Phoenician Women*, 395, quoted by Helmut Koester, "Physis," ed. Gerhard Kittel and Gerhard Friedrich, *Theological Dictionary of the New Testament*, vol. 9 (Grand Rapids, MI: Wm. B. Eerdmans, 1977), 262.

30. Polybius, *Histories*, 15.36, "Greek Texts and Translations," Perseus Under PhiloLogic, http://perseus.uchicago.edu/perseus-cgi/cite query3.pl?dbname=GreekFeb2011&query=Polyb.%2015.36& getid=1.

31. Plutarch, quoted in Mark D. Jordan, *The Ethics of Sex* (Malden, MA: Blackwell, 2002), 33–34.

32. Seneca, *Epistles*, 122.7–8, quoted in John J. Winkler, *The Constraints of Desire: The Anthropology of Sex and Gender in Ancient Greece* (New York: Routledge, 1990), 21; and Craig A. Williams, *Roman Homosexuality*, 2nd ed. (Oxford: Oxford University Press, 2010), 271. Cicero, *De finibus*, 5.35–6, quoted in Williams, *Roman Homosexuality*, 270.

33. For more on this idea, see Brooten, *Love Between Women*, 63, summarizing *The Sentences of Pseudo-Phocylides:* "The author also

---

warns the reader against letting a son have long, braided, or knotted hair, as long hair is for voluptuous women." See also this statement from Roland Barthes, quoted in Anthony C. Thiselton, *The First Epistle to the Corinthians,* The New International Greek Testament Commentary (Grand Rapids, MI: Wm. B. Eerdmans, 2000), 828–29: "Within the semiotic clothing code of first-century Roman society...'a veil or hood constituted a warning: it signified that the wearer was a respectable woman and that no man dare approach her,' i.e., as one potentially or actually sexually 'available.'" See also Dale B. Martin, *The Corinthian Body* (New Haven, CT: Yale University Press, 1995), 229–49.

34. See Brownson, *Bible, Gender, Sexuality,* 204–22.

35. Brownson, *Bible, Gender, Sexuality,* 218.

36. My argument is not limited to the same-sex relationships of gay people. Long-term, monogamous same-sex unions—whether the partners identify as gay, bisexual, pan, queer, or whether they eschew sexual identity labels altogether—are significantly different from the lustful, self-centered behavior Paul has in view in Romans 1:26–27.

37. Along the same lines as Gagnon, New Testament professor Simon Gathercole has made the bigger-picture claim that "the key correspondence" between idolatry and same-sex relations "lies in the fact that both involve turning away from the 'other' to the 'same.'" "Sin in God's Economy: Agencies in Romans 1 and 7" in *Divine and Human Agency in Paul and His Cultural Environment* (London: T&T Clark, 2007), 163–64. But if that analysis were correct, we should expect to see the rest of Romans 1:18–32 fit into that pattern. Yet the exchange of a righteous for a depraved mind in verses 28–32 has nothing to do with "sameness" and difference. Rather, the key correspondence between idolatry and same-sex relations for Paul is that both involve an exchange of order for disorder, and as a result, an exchange of honor for dishonor.

38. See both John Chrysostom's and Augustine's interpretations of the passage, quoted at length in James R. White and Jeffrey D. Niell, *The Same-Sex Controversy: Defending and Clarifying the Bible's*

Message About Homosexuality (Bloomington, MN: Bethany, 2002), 221–47. Chrysostom wrote that Paul "shows that the punishment was in this pleasure itself," 226.

39. Julian of Eclanum, quoted in Augustine, *On Marriage and Concupiscence,* bk. 2, trans. Peter Holmes and Robert Ernest Wallis, rev. Benjamin B. Warfield, in *Nicene and Post-Nicene Fathers,* 1st ser., vol. 5, ed. Philip Schaff (Buffalo, NY: Christian Literature Publishing, 1887), at New Advent, rev. and ed. Kevin Knight, www.new advent.org/fathers/15072.htm.

40. William Sanday and Arthur C. Headlam, *A Critical and Exegetical Commentary on the Epistle to the Romans,* International Critical Commentary, 5th ed. (Edinburgh: T & T Clark, 1902), 50.

Chapter 7

1. See Dale B. Martin, *Sex and the Single Savior: Gender and Sexuality in Biblical Interpretation* (Louisville: Westminster John Knox, 2006), 43–47. Martin wrote, "When used as a term of moral condemnation, the word still refers to something perceived as 'soft': laziness, degeneracy, decadence, lack of courage, or, to sum up all these vices in one ancient category, the feminine," 44.

2. Cicero, *Tusculan Disputations,* 2.53, 55, quoted in Craig A. Williams, *Roman Homosexuality,* 2nd ed. (Oxford: Oxford University Press, 2010), 148.

3. Seneca, *Epistles,* 67.4, quoted in Williams, *Roman Homosexuality,* 151.

4. For more on this idea, see Williams, *Roman Homosexuality,* 145.

5. See Martin, *Sex and the Single Savior,* 44–45.

6. See Peter Brown, "Body and City," in *The Body and Society: Men, Women, and Sexual Renunciation in Early Christianity* (New York: Columbia University Press, 1988); Catharine Edwards, "*Mollitia:* Reading the Body," in *The Politics of Immorality in Ancient Rome* (Cambridge: Cambridge University Press, 2002); and David E. Fredrickson, "Natural and Unnatural Use in Romans 1:24–27: Paul and the Philosophic Critique of Eros," in *Homosexuality, Science, and the "Plain Sense" of Scripture,* ed. David L. Balch (Grand Rapids, MI: Wm. B. Eerdmans, 2000).

7. Plautus, *Truculentus*, 608–11, quoted in Williams, *Roman Homosexuality*, 157–58.

8. Seneca the Elder, *Controversiae*, 2.1.6, quoted in Williams, *Roman Homosexuality*, 163.

9. Plutarch, *Life of Pompey*, 48.5–7, quoted in Edwards, *Politics of Immorality*, 85.

10. See Martin, *Sex and the Single Savior*, 45–46. The detractors of the love of women call it "unmanly," saying that men who are zealous for women show "effeminacy" and "weakness."

11. Fredrickson, "Natural and Unnatural," 197, 218–21. The 1985 New Jerusalem Bible uses a similar translation for *malakos*: "self-indulgent."

12. See Robin Scroggs, *The New Testament and Homosexuality* (Minneapolis: Augsburg Fortress, 1984), 101–9.

13. Martin, *Sex and the Single Savior*, 39.

14. *Sibylline Oracles*, 2.70–77, quoted in Martin, *Sex and the Single Savior*, 40.

15. *Acts of John*, 36, translated in Wilhelm Schneemelcher, ed., *New Testament Apocrypha*, rev. ed., trans. R. McL. Wilson (Philadelphia: Westminster, 1991).

16. Martin, *Sex and the Single Savior*, 42. See Martin's discussion of Hippolytus's *Refutation of All Heresies* and Eusebius's *Preparation for the Gospel*, 42.

17. The word *arsenokoites* reappears in 1 Timothy 1:10, this time in a list of those for whom the law was written:

"Knowing this, that the law is not made for a righteous man, but for the lawless and disobedient, for the ungodly and for sinners, for unholy and profane, for murderers of fathers and murderers of mothers, for manslayers, for whoremongers, for them that defile themselves with mankind [*arsenokoitais*], for menstealers, for liars, for perjured persons, and if there be any other thing that is contrary to sound doctrine" (1 Timothy 1:9–10, KJV).

The linguistic issues in this passage aren't significantly different from those in 1 Corinthians 6:9. The only obvious difference is the absence of the word *malakos,* which undermines the idea that the words *malakos* and *arsenokoites* should be understood as a pair in 1 Corinthians 6. Moreover, in 1 Timothy 1, the term *arsenokoites* appears between a sexual vice ("whoremongers") and a vice of exploitation ("menstealers"), which is similar to its placement in the 1 Corinthians 6 list.

18. That is Robin Scroggs's conclusion in *The New Testament and Homosexuality*, 101–9, 118–20. It's also consistent with the argument of David Fredrickson ("Natural and Unnatural," 218–21). See also James V. Brownson, *Bible, Gender, Sexuality: Reframing the Church's Debate on Same-Sex Relationships* (Grand Rapids, MI: Wm. B. Eerdmans, 2013), 273–75.

19. *Malakos* could possibly be taken to refer to males who take the passive role in same-sex relations, while *arsenokoites* could indicate men who take the active role (albeit in exploitative contexts).

20. As New Testament professor William Loader has written of the word *arsenokoitai*, "The common understanding was that men engaging in such activity were just as likely also to be engaging in sex with women, both licit and illicit." William Loader, *The New Testament on Sexuality: Attitudes Towards Sexuality in Judaism and Christianity in the Hellenistic Greco-Roman Era* (Grand Rapids, MI: Wm. B. Eerdmans, 2012), 332.

Chapter 8

1. John Piper, *This Momentary Marriage: A Parable of Permanence* (Wheaton, IL: Crossway Books, 2009), 179.

2. As Paul explained in Galatians 3:26–29, "In Christ Jesus you are all children of God through faith, for all of you who were baptized into Christ have clothed yourselves with Christ. There is neither Jew nor Greek, neither slave nor free, nor is there male and female, for you are all one in Christ Jesus. If you belong to Christ, then you are Abraham's seed, and heirs according to the promise." In Romans 9:8, too, Paul wrote that "it is not the children by physical descent who are God's children, but it is the children of the promise who are regarded as Abraham's offspring."

3. Piper, *This Momentary Marriage,* 110. Piper drew from the work of theologian Barry Danylak, available in the book *Redeeming Singleness: How the Storyline of Scripture Affirms the Single Life* (Wheaton, IL: Crossway Books, 2010). I am grateful to both Piper and Danylak for many of the insights contained in this section.

4. See James V. Brownson, *Bible, Gender, Sexuality: Reframing the Church's Debate on Same-Sex Relationships* (Grand Rapids, MI: Wm. B. Eerdmans, 2013), 110–26.

5. For a survey of Christian interpretations of Galatians 3:28, see Dale Martin, *Sex and the Single Savior: Gender and Sexuality in Biblical Interpretation* (Louisville: Westminster John Knox, 2006).

6. Robert Gagnon wrote, "Genesis 1 and 2 beautifully image the 'one fleshness' of marriage as a *re*union of an original binary sexual whole. Reconstitution obviously requires the joining of the two constituent parts, male and female, which were the products of the splitting." Dan O. Via and Robert A. J. Gagnon, *Homosexuality and the Bible: Two Views* (Minneapolis: Augsburg Fortress, 2003), 89.

7. See Brownson, *Bible, Gender, Sexuality,* 106.

8. Timothy Keller and Kathy Keller, *The Meaning of Marriage: Facing the Complexities of Commitment with the Wisdom of God* (New York: Dutton, 2011), 223. Both Keller and John Piper oppose same-sex marriage, but as I argue in this chapter, I think the core principles of their beliefs should cause them to reconsider. Andreas Köstenberger made a similar statement about the meaning of the phrase "one flesh" in his book with David W. Jones, *God, Marriage, and Family: Rebuilding the Biblical Foundation* (Wheaton, IL: Crossway Books, 2004), 90: "While 'one flesh' suggests sexual intercourse and normally procreation, at its very heart the concept entails the establishment of a new kinship relationship between two previously unrelated individuals by the most intimate of human bonds."

9. Brownson, *Bible, Gender, Sexuality,* 89.

10. See Brownson, *Bible, Gender, Sexuality,* 101–9. He wrote, "This focus on bonding implicit in becoming one flesh is the basis for the Bible's categorical rejection of all forms of sexual promiscuity.

People are not to say with their bodies what they cannot or will not say with the whole of their lives," 109.

11. I am grateful to Jim Brownson for this observation. See Jim Brownson, "Response to a Review: How to Interpret Ephesians 5," June 11, 2013, http://jimbrownson.wordpress.com/2013/06/11 /response-to-a-review-how-to-interpret-ephesians-5. As Brownson noted, the fact that Jesus has a body similar to ours is important for our affirmation of the incarnation.

12. See David Matzko McCarthy, "The Relationship of Bodies: A Nuptial Hermeneutics of Same-sex Unions," in Eugene F. Rogers Jr., ed., *Theology and Sexuality: Classic and Contemporary Readings* (Malden, MA: Blackwell, 2002), 200–16.

Chapter 9

1. See Anthony A. Hoekema, *Created in God's Image* (Grand Rapids, MI: Wm. B. Eerdmans, 1994), 33–65.

2. Karl Barth, *Church Dogmatics,* vol. 3, pt. 4 (London: T & T Clark, 2004), 166.

3. James B. DeYoung wrote, "It is not possible that male reflects the divine image apart from female.… Homosexuality must affirm that the male gender by itself, or the female gender by itself, is an adequate representation of the divine image." James B. DeYoung, *Homosexuality: Contemporary Claims Examined in Light of the Bible and Other Ancient Literature and Law* (Grand Rapids, MI: Kregel Publications, 2000), 14. Robert Gagnon also has written, " 'Male and female he created them' probably intimates that the fullness of God's 'image' comes together in the union of male and female in marriage (not, one could infer, from same-sex unions)." Robert A. J. Gagnon, *The Bible and Homosexual Practice: Texts and Hermeneutics* (Nashville: Abingdon, 2001), 58.

4. James V. Brownson, *Bible, Gender, Sexuality: Reframing the Church's Debate on Same-Sex Relationships* (Grand Rapids, MI: Wm. B. Eerdmans, 2013), 32.

5. Sirach 17:3–4, though Apocryphal, provides further evidence that ancient Israelites understood the image of God to be related to

humanity's dominion over creation: "God endowed them with strength like his, and he made them according to his image. God made all living beings afraid of them, so that they might exercise dominion over the animals and birds" (CEB).

6. See Dick Staub, *About You: Jesus Didn't Come to Make Us Christian; Jesus Came to Make Us Fully Human* (San Francisco: Jossey-Bass, 2010), 29–37.

7. Hoekema, *Created in God's Image,* 14.

8. Karl Barth, *Church Dogmatics,* vol. 3, pt. 2 (London: T & T Clark, 2004), 324.

9. See C. S. Lewis, *The Great Divorce* (New York: HarperCollins, 2000). I am grateful to Jefferson Bethke for this observation.

10. Barth, *Church Dogmatics,* vol. 3, pt. 4, 116–17.

11. Eugene F. Rogers Jr. makes a detailed argument along these lines in his book *Sexuality and the Christian Body* (Malden, MA: Blackwell, 1999).

12. Linda Robertson, "Just Because He Breathes: Learning to Truly Love Our Gay Son," *Huffington Post,* July 1, 2013, www.huffington post.com/linda-robertson/just-because-he-breathes-learning-to -truly-love-our-gay-son_b_3478971.html.

13. Robertson, "Just Because He Breathes."

14. The book of James further explains that Christian faith should express itself in good deeds, such as caring for widows and orphans (see James 2:14–17). So saving faith in Christ isn't merely a matter of belief. It should be accompanied by repentance from our failings and a desire to do good as we seek to advance God's kingdom on earth (see Matthew 6:10).

15. Eventually, "we shall be like" God, "for we shall see him as he is" (1 John 3:2).

Chapter 10

1. For the biography of a Christian trans woman, see Lisa Salazar, *Transparently: Behind the Scenes of a Good Life* (Vancouver: Lisa S. Salazar, 2011). Also see Jennifer Finney Boylan, *She's Not There: A Life in Two Genders* (New York: Broadway Books, 2013) and *Stuck*

in the Middle with You: A Memoir of Parenting in Three Genders (New York: Crown, 2013). For a detailed theological reflection on transgender issues, see Justin E. Tanis, *Trans-Gendered: Theology, Ministry, and Communities of Faith* (Cleveland, OH: Pilgrim Press, 2003); for both transgender and intersex issues, see Susannah Cornwall, *Sex and Uncertainty in the Body of Christ: Intersex Conditions and Christian Theology* (London: Equinox, 2010). For helpful online resources about trans issues, visit www.thetaskforce .org/issues/transgender, www.transyouthequality.org, and www .transkidspurplerainbow.org.

2. James V. Brownson, *Bible, Gender, Sexuality: Reframing the Church's Debate on Same-Sex Relationships* (Grand Rapids, MI: Wm. B. Eerdmans, 2013), 11. Brownson has done much to clarify this issue for Christians. His book *Bible, Gender, Sexuality* is the first book I would recommend to anyone who wants to continue this conversation at a deeper theological level. Anyone with a basic grasp of Scripture can understand and appreciate his biblical research. For the above quote from his 2005 essay, see James Brownson, "Gay Unions: Consistent Witness or Pastoral Accommodation? An Evangelical Pastoral Dilemma and the Unity of the Church," *Reformed Review* 59, no. 1 (Autumn 2005), www .westernsem.edu/files/1612/8171/5426/Autumn05V59N1.pdf.

3. Justin Lee, *Torn: Rescuing the Gospel from the Gays-vs.-Christians Debate* (New York: Jericho Books, 2012), 77.

4. John Boswell, "Logos and Biography," in Eugene F. Rogers Jr., ed., *Theology and Sexuality: Classic and Contemporary Readings* (Malden, MA: Blackwell, 2002), 359–60.

5. Boswell, "Logos and Biography," 360–61.